The Future Families Project

A Survey of Canadian Hopes and Dreams

University of Lethbridge

FIAT LUX

Reginald W. Bibby

CONTENTS

Acknowledgement

Canadians are fortunately well served by a rich and detailed body of knowledge that describes the fundamental changes that have characterized the patterns of family formation and functioning in recent years. Data collected by Statistics Canada and the scholarship of Canada's academic community has consolidated the knowledge necessary to anyone who needs to know what families look like and how they perform their essential functions to the benefit of their members and the society at large. The numbers provide us with the essential trends that will, in large measure, shape the prospects of individual Canadian children, men and women, and the prospects of the country as a whole.

So we have the facts, but what do they mean? That has been one of the frustrations facing the Vanier Institute of the Family as we are asked for more than just "the facts". With the release of this *Future Families Report*, we can now begin to provide answers to some of the most important questions that we at the VIF are regularly asked and have, until now, been ill-prepared to answer.

Canada will be shaped not only by the trends that are captured by statistical reporting but equally by the reactions, attitudes and opinions of citizens as they strive to understand and adapt to these trends. The prospects of the nation's children will be shaped by the economic, social and community contexts in which they live. And, their prospects will be equally shaped by how well we understand these contexts and how Canadians choose to respond to the issues they reveal. To date, this type of information about how Canadians think and feel about families has fallen far short of what we need to know about the values that guide them as they make personal decisions that carry immense public consequence.

Those who presume to address the present-day challenges of health care and health promotion, housing, child poverty, pension reform, gender equity, welfare reform, tax fairness, post-secondary educational financing and other major policy challenges without taking into account the values and aspirations of Canadian families are going to make misguided choices.

The need to collect and analyze information on the values held by Canadian families was the genesis of this unique VIF project. The Institute appreciates sincerely the financial support provided by Social Development Canada that has made it possible for us to carry out this major national survey on the hopes and dreams of Canadians.

The Institute was also fortunate in being able to call upon the experience and talents of Professor Reginald Bibby of the University of Lethbridge who oversaw the entire project. With his team of researchers, Professor Bibby assumed responsibility for the design of the *Future Families Survey*, the collection of data and its analysis and interpretation. The Institute invited Dr. Bibby to lead this research effort because there is no one in the country better equipped to help us understand how the beliefs and values that Canadians maintain about family life reflect patterns of both profound change and continuity.

Between 1975 and 2000, Dr. Bibby has led a major research effort known as *The Project Canada Research Project*. This program has included six national surveys of adults every five years and national surveys of teenagers in 1984, 1992 and 2000. Designed to complement one another, these surveys represent a rich body of cross-sectional, panel and trend data on life in Canada. Project Canada surveys have not only examined current life experiences pertaining to such topics as marriage and family, but have also explored the values, attitudes, hopes and aspirations of Canadians relative to numerous dimensions of family formation and functioning. Dr Bibby is the author of nine best-selling books and numerous articles, is well respected as a commentator on trends by national and regional media and speaks regularly to a wide variety of audiences across Canada.

The *Future Families Project* was originally conceived and planned by the Vanier Institute's Dr. Robert Glossop who, due to illness and a prolonged period of recovery, withdrew from the project shortly after data collection began. As I express my thanks to him for having launched the project, I also want to acknowledge the special efforts of his staff colleagues who have worked closely with Professor Bibby to bring this report to life. They are Alan Mirabelli, Lisa Dudley, Jennifer Brownrigg, Paula Theetge and Lucie Legault and I acknowledge, with sincere thanks, their unique contributions to the success of this project.

We have also called upon the talents of three other professionals who have regularly supplemented the work of the Vanier Institute staff. We thank Elaine Lowe for her work as editor and Rachelle Renaud and Yannick Morin, our translators, who have provided us with the French version of the text, *Projet familles de demain : Un sondage sur les espoirs et les rêves des Canadiens*.

Whenever Statistics Canada releases a new report on the living circumstances of the Canadian population or the incomes of families or how families spend their money and time, students, researchers, parliamentary committees, community agencies, employers, elected officials, policy-makers, the media and family members themselves want to know: What do these statistical trends mean? What are the values that lie behind the behaviors and decisions reflected in all these numbers? Are Canadians concerned about what they see happening?

It is our pleasure to share the answers to some of these questions with you with this publication of our *Future Families Report,* and we invite you to share your comments on this study by posting your observations on our guestbook, located on our website at www.vifamily.ca.

Allan D. MacKay
President

Introduction

Background

In the summer of 2002, Robert Glossop, Executive Director of Programs and Research for the Vanier Institute of the Family in Ottawa, contacted sociologist Reginald Bibby of the University of Lethbridge, to explore the possibility of carrying out a collaborative national survey. Glossop maintained that, as a result of the data generated by Statistics Canada and researchers across the country, we know a fair amount about the changing nature and functions of families—the forms families have been taking and how people have been adapting.

However, Glossop contended that our information base on families lacks an up-to-date reading of family aspirations—what Canadians hope to experience and are encouraged to experience. Such a reading, he maintained, is essential to clear perception, policy formulation and practical responses. In short, there would be value in carrying out a national survey that would offer a clear understanding of what people actually want from family life.

Bibby too felt that such a survey might have considerable worth and agreed to oversee the project, including the data analysis, and summary report. Planning for the survey began in the fall of 2002.

The Survey

The project became known as **The Future Families Project**. A questionnaire was constructed with the project's primary objective in mind—to get a thorough national reading on the ideal versus the real—what Canadians want from family life compared to what they report they have experienced. To be thorough, the questionnaire was organized into sections dealing with key facets of family life—the nature of the family; dating; sexuality and cohabitation; marriage; children, parenting and parents; and separation and divorce. It also included sections exploring Canadians' thoughts on how family life might be enhanced—what areas warrant particular priority, who is responsible for realizing these priorities, and who should share in the actual costs. A large number of background independent variables were included to permit extensive analyses of the data, both now and in the future. The 11-page questionnaire had a total of 445 variables. Drafts were scrutinized by Vanier Institute personnel as well as by academics in both Canada and the United States.[1]

The sample is unique. It was designed to consist of: (1) people who had participated in Professor Bibby's **Project Canada** national surveys conducted every five years from 1975 through 2000 (thus generating panel data) and (2) new respondents. The objective was to procure a sample of more than 2,000 people, fairly evenly balanced between panel members and newcomers. During fall 2003 and early 2004, the addresses of panel participants were updated and a sample of potential new participants drawn, the latter with telephone directories as the sampling frame.

[1] We are indebted to a number of people for their feedback on the questionnaire, including Robert Brym, Donald Swenson, Diane Clark, Diane Erickson, Kelly Cardwell, James Penner and Armand Mauss.

Data collection was carried out by mail over about a five-month period spanning March 15 to August 15, 2003. A total of 2,093 adults eighteen and over participated in the survey. There were about 900 people who had participated in previous Project Canada surveys and 1,200 new respondents. The latter included roughly 300 people, mostly under the age of 35, who were added as a quota sample to ensure the participation of a good cross-section of younger adults.

With appropriate weighting for variables such as province, community size, gender, age, and—in the case of the quota sample–religion, the sample is highly representative of Canadian adults.[2] A sample of this size should permit accurate generalizations to the national population within approximately 2.5 percentage points, 19 times in 20.

	Population	**Sample**
British Columbia	13%	14
Alberta	10	9
Saskatchewan	3	4
Manitoba	4	4
Ontario	38	37
Quebec	24	24
New Brunswick	2	2
Nova Scotia	3	3
Prince Edward Island	<1	<1
Newfoundland-Labrador	2	2
North	<1	<1
100,000-plus	60	59
99,000-10,000	13	15
under 10,000	27	26
Female	51	51
Male	49	49
18-34	30	28
35-54	41	42
55 and over	29	30
Married	58	57
Never married	24	21
Cohabiting	9	12
Widowed	6	5
Divorced	3	5

[2] Some differences reflect rounding of numbers, versus significant substantive variations. Marital status for the population is estimated from Statistics Canada, *Cansim*, table 051-0010 and catalogue no. 95F0506XCB01009.

The Nature of the Family

What's a Family

We started our investigation by trying to get a sense of how Canadians personally view the family.[1] Our intent was to go beyond a reading of what people are willing to accept or tolerate to an understanding of what they themselves believe to be families. ***"Apart from official definitions," we asked, "which of the following arrangements do you yourself see as constituting 'a family'?"*** We posed nine configurations that incorporated three variables: marital status, children and sexual orientation.

- Almost all Canadians (96%) see a married man and woman with at least once child as a family.
- The presence of a child is part of the perception of family units for most people: 7 in 10 see unmarried or divorced and separate parents as families, while 6 in 10 say the same about a single parent. The figure drops to 5 in 10 in the case of same-sex parents.
- About 3 in 10 Canadians see cohabiting couples with no children as families, with the figure dropping to just over 2 in 10 when the couples are gay.
- Only 1 in 10 view a single person with no children as constituting a family.

There are striking differences by age.

- Younger adults are far more inclined than older adults to see the family as taking on an array of forms.
- Nonetheless, the options for what constitutes a family are ranked the same, regardless of age. Among adults under the age of 35, about 1 in 3 see unmarried couples with no children as families, and about the same proportion view single persons with no children as families.

These findings indicate that the so-called "traditional family" [2] is the family form most widely recognized by Canadians. However, other forms are also seen as families by significant numbers of people.

Table 1.1. Views of What Constitutes a Family by Age

% Indicating "Yes"

	Nationally	18-34	35-54	55+
A married man and woman with at least one child	96%	97	97	95
An unmarried man and woman with at least one child	68	82	71	48
A divorced or separated person with at least one child	68	80	71	52
An unmarried person with at least one child	61	77	65	40
A married man and woman with no children	56	64	55	49
Two people of the same sex with at least one child	46	68	45	24
An unmarried man and woman with no children	33	36	34	28
Two people of the same sex with no children	24	35	22	15
One single person with no children	9	8	10	9

Family Experiences Growing Up

We next asked, *"Which of these [nine family arrangements] best describes your family when you were growing up?"*

- Ninety per cent indicated that they came from homes where their parents were married.
- Another 4% said their parents were separated or divorced.
- About 2% informed us their parents had not been married.
- The remaining 4% said they had come from other home settings (e.g., blended families, widowed or gay parents); none of these family types reached 1%.
- **People under the age of 35** were somewhat less likely than others to report that their parents had been married when they were growing up, and slightly more likely to indicate they had been divorced or separated.

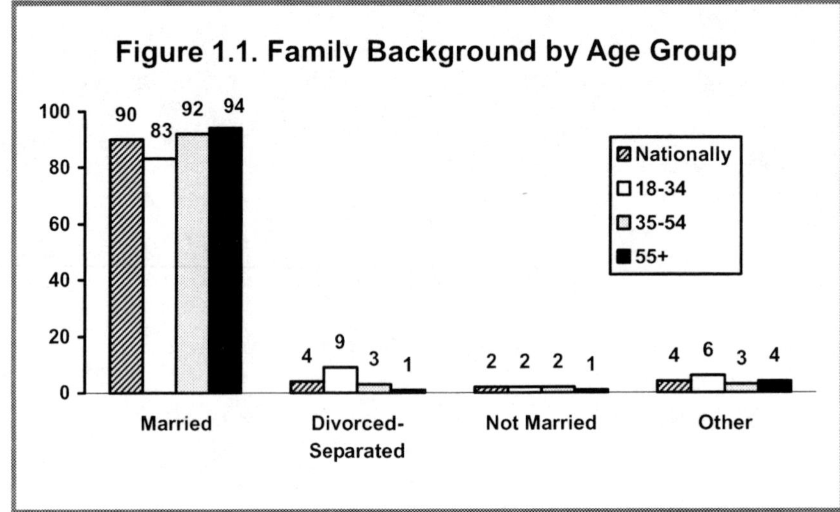

The fact that about 90% of Canadians had married parents masks some of the configurations involved. When asked more specifically who "primarily" raised them, 84% of Canadians indicated their mother and father.

- About 9% say they were raised primarily by their mother and 1% were raised by their father.
- Another 2% indicate they were raised by their mother and stepfather; 1% were raised by adoptive parents; and about 1% by their mother or father and another individual.
- The remainder report other parental combinations.

Table 1.2. Roles of One's Parents

Who primarily raised you?

Mother & father	84%
Mother only	9
Mother & stepfather	2
Adoptive parents	1
Father only	1
Father & stepmother	<1
Mother & male partner	<1
Father & female partner	<1
Other	2

Current Family Situations

We also asked our respondents, *"Which of these [nine family arrangements] best describes your current family situation?"* The question differs from the "family growing up" question in that it includes many single people, for example, as well as older people who may be widowed or have children who no longer are alive.

That said,

- More than two in four Canadian adults report being part of traditional families
- Another one in four are either single or married individuals with no children.
- Most of the remaining one in four are divorced and separated parents (5%), unmarried parents (5%), and unmarried couples with no children (5%); smaller numbers of people are single parents, or gays and lesbians with no children (2% each).

Variations by age are fairly predictable. They seem to reflect life stage rather than any significant generational differences in family structure choices.

- For example, among 18-to-34-year-olds, 73% are either married with or without children, or single without children; the comparable figure for those 35 to 54 is 76%.
- Both figures are lower than those for people 55 and over (83%), primarily due to higher levels of cohabitation.

What is worth watching is whether or not these higher levels of cohabitation among younger adults persist. If they do, it could signal a permanent change in family form choices. If they decrease as people who are currently cohabiting marry, it would suggest that cohabitation is primarily pre-marital and inter-marital in nature.

This initial "aerial shot" of the family composition of Canada will become clearer as we look at more detailed information on marriage, divorce, parenthood and aging.[3]

Table 1.3. Current Family Situation by Age

% Indicating "Yes"

	Nationally	18-34	35-54	55+
A married man and woman with at least one child	53%	38	60	61
A single person with no children	14	24	9	11
A married man and woman with no children	9	11	7	11
A divorced or separated person with at least one child	7	6	9	6
An unmarried man and woman with at least one child	5	6	5	2
An unmarried man and woman with no children	5	11	2	2
An unmarried person with at least one child	2	1	2	1
Two people of the same sex with no children	2	1	3	1
Two people of the same sex with at least one child	<1	<1	<1	<1
Other	3	2	2	5
TOTALS	100	100	100	100

Is There One Ideal Family Form?

The initial findings concerning what Canadians see as families and their own family situations past and present can lead to two early assumptions: (1) people who recognize the conventional family as a family also see it as the ideal family form, and (2) the kind of family life people have experienced is what they really want–that is, the situations in which they are in have matched their family dreams. However, both assumptions are precarious.

In probing the merits of those assumptions **we asked our respondents, *"Do you find any ONE of these [nine] family arrangements to be IDEAL?"***

- Fifty-eight per cent indicated that they believe that the traditional family arrangement is ideal–a married man and woman with at least one child.

- Another 40% said, "No," they do not think that any one single form is ideal.

- The remaining 2% maintained that any of the other eight family arrangements are "ideal."

Figure 1.2 One Ideal Family Form?

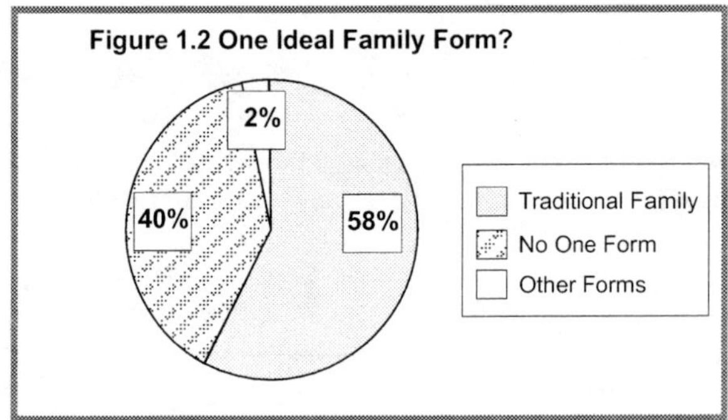

There are noteworthy differences by a number of variables, including region, gender, age, education, religious service attendance and sexual orientation.

- The traditional family is seen as ideal by slightly higher proportions of people on the *Prairies* (67%) and in the *Atlantic* provinces (63%) than elsewhere; residents of *British Columbia* are the least likely to see the traditional family as ideal (47%) and the most likely to maintain there is no one ideal family (53%).

- The conventional family ideal is expressed by slightly more males than females, *older adults* than younger, and by people with less than a *university education* versus those with university degrees.

- The traditional family as ideal is held by about 3 in 4 people who attend *religious services weekly*, and by 2 in 4 who do not.

- The traditional family is seen as the ideal family form *by about* 60% of *heterosexuals*, compared to about 20% of *gays and lesbians*.

- Racially, couples from mixed racial *backgrounds* are somewhat more likely than others to not see any arrangement as ideal.

Table 1.4. Ideal Family Views by Select Variables

Do you find a ny ONE of these family arrangements to be IDEAL?

	Traditional	Other	No	Totals
Nationally	**58%**	**2**	**40**	**100**
Prairies	67	1	32	100
Atlantic	63	2	35	100
Ontario	60	1	39	100
Quebec	56	4	40	100
BC	47	<1	53	100
Males	63	2	35	100
Females	54	1	45	100
55+	74	2	24	100
35-54	56	3	41	100
18-34	48	<1	52	100
Some PS	68	2	30	100
HS or Less	60	2	38	100
Univ Grads	52	1	47	100
Weeklys	78	1	21	100
Less Weekly	52	2	46	100
Heterosexuals	59	1	40	100
Gays & Lesbians	21	10	69	100
Partners White	64	2	34	100
Other	78	2	20	100
Mixed	58	0	42	100

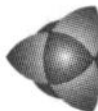

Examining the question of "one family ideal" by respondents' current family situation sheds some light on the merits of the second assumption noted earlier–that what people have experienced in the way of family life is what they really want.

- Almost 70% of married parents with children say the traditional family is the ideal; that leaves most of the remaining 30% who do not think there is just one ideal family form.

- However, approximately 1 in 2 unmarried parents also express the conventional family ideal, as do 1 in 2 unmarried couples without children—both heterosexual and gay.

- About 1 in 3 Canadians living in other family arrangements—including those who are married without children and those who are divorced or separated—endorse the traditional family model, while 2 in 3 say there is no ideal family form.

- Of considerable importance, when thinking of one ideal family arrangement, relatively few people advocate any option beyond the traditional family. Less than 1% of those who are unmarried with children, for example, say they think that arrangement is "the ideal family form." Similarly, while 47% of cohabiting couples without children see the traditional model as ideal, just 2% give the same "ideal family form" rating to being unmarried parents or to being married without children.

In short, about 6 in 10 Canadians see the traditional family as the ideal family arrangement, while most of the remaining 4 in 10—led by younger adults—take the position that there is no one ideal form. Although many people find a variety of family forms that work for them, relatively few put forward any specific alternative as ideal beyond the traditional family.

Table 1.5. Belief There Is One Ideal Family Arrangement by One's Own Current Family Situation

"Do you find any ONE of these family arrangements to be IDEAL?

Own Current Family Situation	Nuclear	Other	No	Totals
A married man and woman with at least one child	68%	1	31	100
An unmarried man and woman with at least one child	52	2	46	100
Two people of the same sex with no children	49	1	50	100
An unmarried man and woman with no children	47	6	47	100
A married man and woman with no children	36	5	59	100
A single person with no children	33	2	65	100
A divorced or separated person with at least one child	31	0	69	100
Two people of the same sex with at least one child	27	9	64	100
An unmarried person with at least one child	***	***	***	***
Other	59	1	40	100

***Insufficient number of cases to permit stable percentaging.

Who's in the Family

People perceive their significant family members in various ways, exhibiting varying levels of inclusiveness. Age is strongly related to who is part of our families at specific points in time.

We asked Canadians, *"Who, at this point in your life, comprises YOUR family?"* We offered 15 possibilities, and invited respondents to add others.

- Nationally, *brothers* and *sisters* are the most widely cited family members (73%), followed next by *partners* and *children* (63%).
- What happened to mom and dad? For many people, especially those who are older, their parents are no longer alive.
- Mothers are cited as comprising the families of 57% of Canadians and fathers cited by 44%.
- About 50% cited other people, including nieces, nephews, cousins, aunts and uncles.
- In-laws are part of the families of about 1 in 4 Canadians, while grandchildren are family members for some 1 in 5 people—including more than 40% of those 55 and over.
- Each of stepmothers, stepfathers and stepsiblings are family members for roughly 5% of the population.

Table 1.6. Reported Family Members

"Who, at this point in your life, comprises YOUR family?"

	Nat	18-34	35-54	55+
Your brother(s) &/or sister(s)	73	82	73	63
Your partner	63	52	73	69
Your children/child	63	27	76	78
Your mother	57	87	61	21
Your niece(s) &/or nephew(s)	53	41	58	55
Your cousin(s)	50	59	47	47
Your aunt(s) &/or uncle(s)	46	61	46	30
Your father	44	77	47	10
Your mother-in-law	31	32	42	15
Your father-in-law	23	29	31	7
Your grandparent(s)	22	53	14	4
Your grandchildren/grandchild	18	3	11	43
Your stepmother	5	6	6	2
Your stepfather	5	10	4	1
Your stepbrother(s) &/or sister(s)	6	8	5	4
Other	8	13	6	5

A possible trend worth noting is that just over 3% of young adults list friends as comprising their families, an inclination less common among 35-to-54-year-olds and quite uncommon among adults 55 and over.

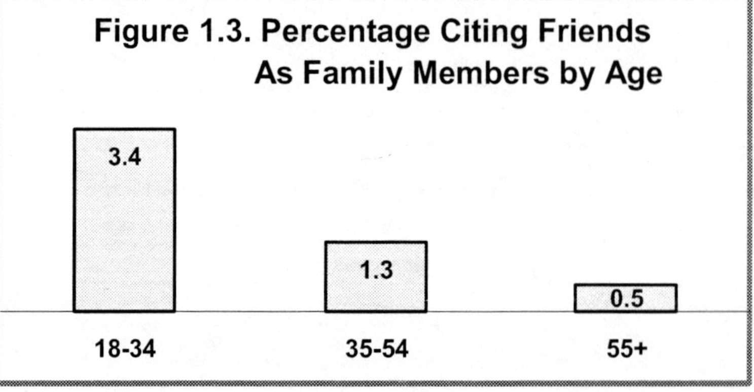

How Important is the Family?

Canadians have differences of opinion about what constitutes a family and whether or not one family arrangement is better than another. However, they are nearly unanimous in emphasizing the importance of the family.

- 97% say that the family is essential to personal well-being.
- 97% also agree that the family is essential to instill values that are needed for interpersonal life.
- 95% say the family is essential to healthy communities.
- 95% also think the family is essential to a healthy nation.

Table 1.7. Importance of Families

Families are important because they are essential to..."

% Strongly Agreeing or Agreeing

	Nat	18-34	35-54	55+
Personal well-being	97	96	97	98
The instilling of values required for interpersonal life	97	97	97	98
Healthy communities	95	92	96	99
A healthy nation	95	92	95	98
Canadas strength and vitality	94	89	94	98

With respect to the latter, in 1967, Canada's Centennial Year, Prime Minister Lester B. Pearson said that he believed "the strengthening of family life in Canada [was] the basis on which our nation's moral strength and vitality depend." We repeated this statement in the survey, and asked Canadians what they thought.

- 46% said they strongly agree with the former Prime Minister
- 48% indicated they agree
- 6% said they disagree
- fewer than 1% said they strongly disagree.

Table 1.8.
The Top Five Things People Say Family Adds to Their Lives

1. Love	29%
2. Support	13
3. Stability	9
4. Happiness	9
5. Companionship	8

In probing what the family means to people across the country, we asked, *"What is the single most important thing your family adds to your life?"* The top five responses in descending order were: companionship, happiness, stability, support and—number one—love.

Mothers and fathers have been central to family life for the majority of Canadians. For the most part, they are viewed as having been good role models, though not perfect.

"What is the Single Most Important Thing Your Family Adds to Your Life?"
Some Response Examples

...love...stable support...being needed...joy...a sense of belonging...peace...closeness ...well-being...group spirit...structure...reasons to live...forgiveness...it is always there for me...a place of safety...cohesion...incentive to go on...stability...caring...spending days off not being stressed out...security...unconditional support...a sense of completion... membership...pride...purpose...solidarity...their staying in contact...the giving and receiving of love...companionship...humour...richness that is not based on money...responsibility ...happiness...life itself...positive unconditional acceptance...fulfillment...historical continuity...togetherness... at 69 my family is my society...sharing...a sense of identity ...respect...contentment...

- More than 9 in 10 people say their mothers provided them with *a good model for family life generally*, and just over 8 in 10 say the same thing about their fathers.

- The figures slip slightly for moms and dads when the question is raised about their having been *good models for raising children*.

- The numbers slip a bit further when respondents are asked if their parents provided *good models for marriage*—to 77% for mothers and 72% for fathers. This also means that 1 in 4 Canadians *do not* think their parents provided good marriage role models.

Table 1.9. Parents as Good Models

My mother/father provided me with a good model for..."

% Strongly Agreeing or Agreeing

		Nat	18-34	35-54	55+
Family life generally	Mother	92%	91	91	93
	Father	83	82	82	88
Raising children	Mother	88	88	85	91
	Father	77	77	74	83
Marriage	Mother	77	72	75	86
	Father	72	66	69	82

- Positive sentiments about the modelling parents provided tend to be slightly higher overall among people 55 and over, versus those 35 to 54 or 18 to 34. In generational language, the above three age groups essentially correspond to "pre-Boomers," "Boomers" and "Gen-Xers" respectively. In this instance, the pre-Boomers tend to hold somewhat more favourable views of their parents' performances than Boomers or Gen-Xers.

A Quick Family Facts Postscript

The survey offers a few additional findings worth noting.

- **Families are getting smaller.** The decreasing number of both siblings and children reported by younger adults corroborates a well-documented decline in family size.[4]

- **Families frequently include older children, and in some instances, parents and grandparents.** Some 1 in 3 adults between 18 and 29 say they are living with their parents.[5] About 1 in 20 adult households include a parent and/or a grandparent.[6]

Some families face unique challenges: 7% of parents report that their children have special needs. Usually they are younger children; in some instances they are adults.[7]

Table 1.10. Some Family Facts

	NAT	18-34	35-54	55+
Average (mean) number of...				
siblings	2.7	1.8	3.1	3.1
children	2.4	1.7	2.2	2.8
people in your residence	2.7	2.8	3.0	2.0
% Residing with Parents				
offspring 18-29	33	33	---	---
% Of Households...				
with parent/grandparent who has resided for > one year	4	4	6	2
% Of Parents...				
offspring have special needs	7	3	8	5

THE LONGER LOOK

The Future of the Traditional Family: 1975-2000

	1975	1980	1985	1990	1995	2000
Will gain influence	15%	24	32	35	28	21
Will lose influence	38	51	42	44	44	61
Will remain about the same	47	25	26	21	28	18

Source: Reginald W. Bibby, Project Canada Survey Series.

Summary Note

About 90% of Canadian adults indicate that they were raised in homes where they had two married parents. However, things have been changing. The traditional family pattern—while still dominant— has been somewhat less prevalent among younger adults than their older counterparts. Cohabitation is fairly common, as is parenthood among unmarried couples.

So it is that while Canadians are close to unanimous in seeing "two married parents" as a family, large numbers extend the notion of family well beyond these traditional parameters. About 60% of Canadians—led by older adults—maintain that the ideal kind of family is "a married man and woman with at least one child"; roughly 40%—led by younger adults—opt for a pluralistic view of the family, asserting that there is "no one family ideal." However, very few people advocate any family arrangement other than the conventional model as ideal, regardless of their own personal family situations.

While parents are central to family life for most Canadians, the national "snapshot" of family life reveals that siblings are the most common component of family life at any one point in time. Regardless of the forms the family is seen to take, it continues to be seen as having paramount importance. Canadians view families as essential to personal and social well-being. The family is viewed as a key source of love, support, stability, happiness and companionship, and as fundamental to optimum community and national life.

Next we look at some specific components of family life, beginning with "how it all starts."

Reflections
How Canadians conceptualize family

The realities of divorce, cohabitation, couples without children and gay relationships have led many observers—particularly academics and journalists—to assume that "there is no such thing as the Canadian family—just Canadian families." Along the way, the notion of "the perfect family with two parents and 2.5 children" has been more than occasionally maligned and dismissed as antiquated. Such a polemical argument has contributed to the perception that Canadians have no ideal structure in mind when it comes to the family, and that family configuration options are pretty much "up for grabs."

The survey findings point to a very different conclusion. **The traditional family with its two parents and one or more children continues to be by far the most widely recognized family form.** Smaller majorities of respondents—led by younger adults—also view households in which children are present as families. However, the belief that other arrangements are families progressively decreases when referring to (a) married heterosexual couples with no children, (b) same-sex couples with children, and (c) other couples with no children. Single individuals who do not have children are viewed by relatively few people as families.

Particularly telling is the finding that, when asked if there is one ideal family arrangement, most Canadians cite either "the traditional family or nothing." That is to say that about six in ten people see the conventional family as ideal while most of the remaining four in ten take "a pluralistic posture," indicating that there is no one ideal form. Although different family forms are acknowledged and accepted, very few people indicate that common-law relationships or single parenthood represent ideal family arrangements.

As for the key players in family life, mothers, fathers and children are central for most people. Yet, at any given point in time, they actually are outnumbered by links to siblings. In the midst of Mother's Day, Father's Day, and Children's Day celebrations, entrepreneurs have missed the most pervasive family link of all—existing ties that Canadians have to their sisters and brothers.

Mothers and to a slightly lesser extent fathers receive generally favourable reviews for how they modelled their family roles to their children. **What's not at all in doubt is the ongoing importance that Canadians give to families.** For almost everyone, the significance of families extends beyond how they shape individuals and their personal relationships. Most Canadians believe firmly that families are important foundations of our communities and, indeed, of the nation as a whole.

In 1975, we found that 38% of Canadians felt the traditional family would lose influence in the future. By 2000, that figure had jumped to 61%. Such findings are consistent with widespread media and academic proclamations about the demise of the traditional family. **What our current findings indicate is that, beyond their perception of what is taking place, Canadians across the country continue to view the traditional family as the most recognizable and most preferred family form.** Obviously we have a mosaic of family structures in Canada. However, the largest tile within that mosaic continues to occupied by the nuclear family.

Some Issues Raised by the Findings

1. Is it desirable or even possible to devise ways of supporting Canadians as they pursue their aspiration to live in a traditional family?

2. Would policies and practices in support of this conventional family aspiration disparage other family forms or the individuals who, either by choice or circumstance, live in them?

3. Given the importance Canadians place on family life generally, what can be done to enhance family life in all its varied forms?

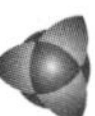

Dating, Sexuality and Cohabitation

Dating and Going Out

The term "dating" in some ways sounds passé. According to popular mythology, older Canadians paired up and then participated in groups, whereas younger Canadians participate in groups and then pair up. *"Do you want to go out with me?"* has been replaced with, *"Do you want to hang out with us?"* The image of an individual suitor with a box of chocolates has been replaced by the image of a group of friends.

The survey findings, while not challenging the use of the term "dating," raise serious doubts about the assumption that a movement from the individual to the group has taken place. When we look at Pre-Boomers (born before about 1950), Baby Boomers (born between about 1950 and 1970), and Generation-Xers (born since around 1970), we actually find the opposite of what we expected.

- Some 82% of Pre-Boomers report that as teenagers, "We didn't so much date as we hung out in groups."
- That claim is made by smaller majorities of 77% of Boomers and 70% of Gen-Xers.

The teenage years for Pre-Boomers spanned roughly the 1940s, 50s and early 60s. Boomers were teens in the late 60s and 70s, and Gen-Xers in the 80s and 90s. Our findings suggest that while older Canadians may have "dated" more, such one-on-one rituals were still secondary to group activities — perhaps even more so than in recent years.

What hasn't changed much is the age at which Canadians have begun "dating" or "going out." Moreover, there is solid consensus about the ideal age to start.

- Older adults report that, on average, they started dating or going when they were 17; they are inclined to think the ideal age is a *bit younger*.
- Middle-age adults tend to see the average age they started dating as the ideal age—a little over 16.
- Younger adults on average say that they started going out/dating just before they turned 16; they think the ideal age is a *bit older*.

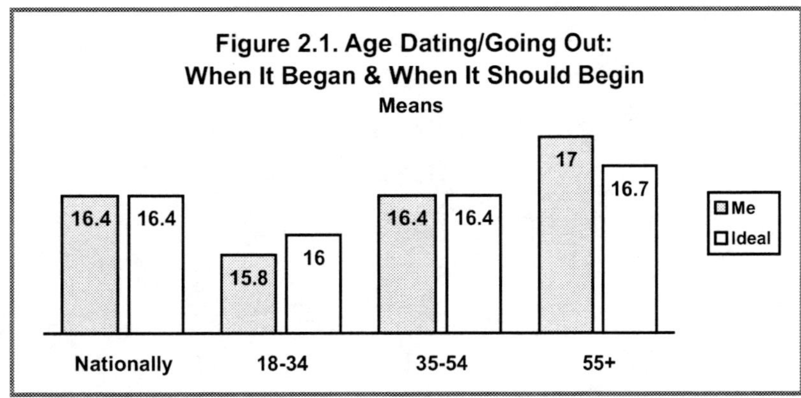

What People Want in a Partner

We asked our respondents, *"What would you say are the TWO most important characteristics a person should look for in a partner?"*

- The solid number one response is *honesty*—sometimes expressed with related words such as "trust" or "faithfulness."
- Securely in second place is *kindness*, variously cited using similar words including "compassion" and "caring."
- *Respect* is number three and *compatibility* number four.
- The fifth through eighth most desirable characteristics are *humour*, *dependability*, *love* and *values*—with the latter expressed by terms such as "good values" and "moral character."
- The final two characteristics are *religious commonality* and *communication*.

Table 2.1.
The Top Ten Characteristics One Should Look for in a Partner

Characteristic	%
1. Honesty	50%
2. Kindness	15
3. Respect	11
4. Compatibility	10
5. Humour	9
6. Dependability	9
7. Love	8
8. Values	8
9. Religious Commonality	7
10. Communication	6

The rankings of these desirable characteristics tend to differ little by gender or age. Honesty and kindness are the top two characteristics for each cohort. Minor variations in the top five characteristics cited include:

- *men* rank compatibility higher than *women*, and respect lower.
- *younger adults* rank humour higher and love lower than *older adults*.

Table 2.2
The Top Five Characteristics One Should Look for in a Partner By Gender and Age

Nationally	Women	Men
1. Honesty	1. Honesty	1. Honesty
2. Kindness	2. Kindness	2. Compatibility
3. Respect	3. Respect	3. Kindness
4. Compatibility	4. Humour	4. Values
5. Humour	5. Dependability	5. Love
18-34	**35-54**	**55+**
1. Honesty	1. Honesty	1. Honesty
2. Kindness	2. Kindness	2. Kindness
3. Respect	3. Respect	3. Compatibility
4. Humour	4. Dependability	4. Love
5. Compatibility	5. Humour	5. Dependability

"What would you say are the TWO most important characteristics a person should look for in a partner?"
Some Response Examples

...trustworthy...loyalty of friendship...kindness...same interests and goals...autonomy... ability to love...family values...character...self-reliance...maturity...sexual attraction ...similar faith...patience...brains... friendship...self-esteem...being responsible... communication...integrity...caring...health...ability to provide security...truthfulness... education...morals...looks...faithfulness...dependability...understanding...independent outlook...considerate...honesty...personality...respect...non-smoker...consistency ...compassion...supportive....love... compatibility...similar values...physical chemistry ...similar interests...common goals...sense of humour...appearance...common sense ...fidelity...mental stability...intelligence...compatible...ambition...understanding... financial stability...similar values...hard working...similar beliefs...listening skills...

Sexual Information

The survey asked Canadians about the sources of their information about sex. Four main groups of sources were identified.

- The *top* information sources are *friends and books*—cited by about 60% of respondents.

- The *second* set of sources consists of other *media*, including the Internet and **school courses**—noted by some 30 to 40%.

- The *third* source is *family members*–led by mothers (22%), followed by siblings (16%), and fathers (10%).

- The *fourth* information sources acknowledged are *religious groups* (5%) and *partners/spouses* (7%).

There are few sizeable differences in the sources cited by women compared to men.

- **Slightly more *men* than women say magazines, movies and the Internet were important sources of sexual information.**

- ***Women* are considerably more likely than men to say that their mothers were an important source of information (30% vs. 14%).**

- ***Men* are slightly more likely than women to point out that their fathers were a key information source (13% vs. 7%). However, this relative difference should not obscure the important finding that fathers are not seen a major source of sexual information by very many Canadians, young or old.**

Table 2.3. Sources of Sexual Information by Age

"To what extent did you learn about sexuality from the following?"

% Indicating A Great Deal or Quite A Bit

	Nationally	Women	Men	18-34	35-54	55+
Your friends	60%	61	60	72	58	51
Books	59	61	58	54	63	61
Television	39	37	40	58	35	19
Magazines	37	32	41	42	36	30
The Internet	36	32	41	42	36	30
School courses	34	37	31	52	30	17
Movies	32	28	36	49	29	14
Your mother	22	30	14	32	17	19
Your brother(s) &/or sister(s)	16	17	16	18	15	17
Your father	10	7	13	16	7	8
Religious groups/leaders	7	8	7	6	6	11
Other *(write-in)*: partner/spouse	5	4	5	3	6	5

* Here and in subsequent tables, shading indicates variable differences of 10 percentage points or more.

Have these information sources changed over time? An examination of the sources by age reveals that the rank order is fairly similar for Gen-Xers, Boomers and Pre-Boomers.

- What's different is that greater proportions of adults under the age of 35—followed by adults 35 to 54—are inclined to cite *almost all* of these sources as having contributed "a great deal" or "quite a bit" to their knowledge of sexuality.

- We are not only talking about the media: nearly twice as many younger adults than older adults report that they learned about sex from their mothers and fathers. Books, religious groups, siblings and partners/spouses are exceptions to this pattern.

- As sex has become more overt in the media, in school courses and in personal lives—including the lives of mothers and fathers—the amount of sex information being passed along existing and newer pathways such as the Internet has increased dramatically.

This greater openness about sex is reflected in the responses we received when we asked our sample, *"Do you—or did you, or do you plan to—talk about sexuality with your children?"* About 88% said either, "Yes, a fair amount" or "Yes, a bit." Only 3% replied, "No, not at all."

- However, 66% of 18- to- 34-year-olds indicated, "Yes, a fair amount" compared to 57% of 35-to 54-year-olds and only 35% of adults 55 and over.

- That may merely reflect good intentions. But it also appears to reflect greater openness about sex on the part of parents. The results show in what 18- to- 34-year-olds report about sexual learning from their mothers and fathers.

Figure 2.2. Discussing Sexuality With One's Children

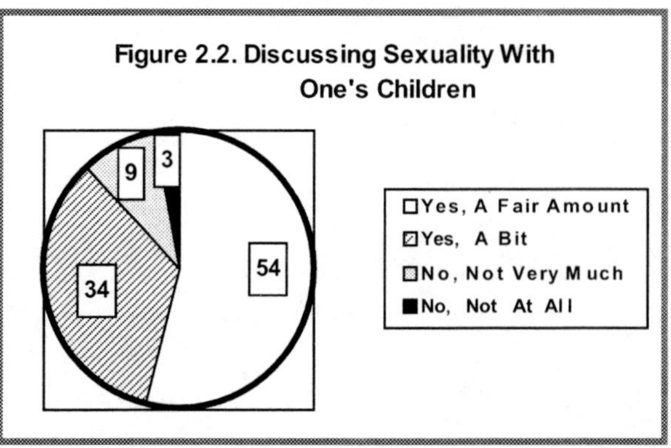

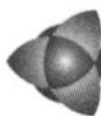

Across Canada, the inclination to discuss sexuality with one's children is fairly even.

- *Quebec's* apparent greater reluctance to do so is tied to the past ("did you") rather than the present or future: 62% of Quebec adults under 35 say they plan to talk "a fair amount" about sexuality to their children, compared to 47% of those 35 to 54, and only 33% of adults 55 and older. The secularization of Quebec has been bringing sex out into the open, in sharp contrast to the pre-1960s.

Table 2.4. Discussing Sexuality by Age and Region

"Do you – or did you, or do you plan to – talk about sexuality with your children?"

	A Fair Amount	A Bit	Little/ None	Totals
Nationally	**54%**	**34**	**12**	**100**
18-34	66	31	3	100
35-54	57	33	10	100
55+	35	39	26	100
Atlantic	60	28	12	100
BC	57	32	11	100
Prairies	57	32	11	100
Ontario	54	33	13	100
Quebec	47	41	12	100
18-34	*62*	*34*	*4*	*100*
35-54	*47*	*42*	*11*	*100*
55+	*33*	*48*	*19*	*100*

These strong differences between generations can further be seen when we look at gender, education and religious service attendance. In the case of each of these three variables, age is *inversely* associated with talking about sexuality with one's children. In other words, the older the person, the less inclined they are to talk with their children about sexuality.

- For example—assuming that age has to do with era and not just life-cycle—we can see that, in the past, *women* have shown more openness toward discussing sexuality with their children than men. With time, women have become even more open to such discussions. However, so have men, with the result that the gender gap has closed considerably.

- Similarly, people have shown a greater tendency to broach the topic of sex with their offspring, regardless of *education*. Only in recent years—as seen in adults under 35— has education been directly associated with a greater inclination to have such conversations.

- People who *attend religious services* every week have not differed much in their tendencies to discuss sexuality with their children from those who attend less often. However, younger adults in both categories do differ considerably from older adults in being far more inclined to talk about sex with their children.

Table 2.5. Discussing Sexuality by Gender, Education & Service Attendance

Do you or did you, or do you plan to talk about sexuality with your children?

% Indicating A Fair Amount

	Nat	18-34	35-54	55+
Nationally	**54**	**66%**	**57**	**35**
Females	62	68	68	44
Males	45	63	46	27
Univ Grads	57	74	58	29
Some PS	55	58	59	43
HS or Less	49	58	54	36
Less Weekly	55	66	55	36
Weekly	52	64	65	35

In all three instances, age is more important than gender, education and religious service attendance by themselves.

An examination of the item by sexual orientation reveals that gays and lesbians are considerably more likely than heterosexuals to indicate that sexuality is something they have discussed or would discuss "a fair amount" with their children. The finding would seem to be obvious, given the minority status of homosexuality in Canadian society.

- For example, older gays with children and younger ones who might adopt them would undoubtedly find themselves having to discuss sexuality with their children.

This also means that about 3 in 10 gays and lesbians did not or do not plan to talk about sex "a fair amount" with their offspring.

- However, age is key: more than 9 in 10 gays and lesbians under the age of 35 say they have had or will have such conversations—considerably higher than the 5 in 10 level for their older counterparts.

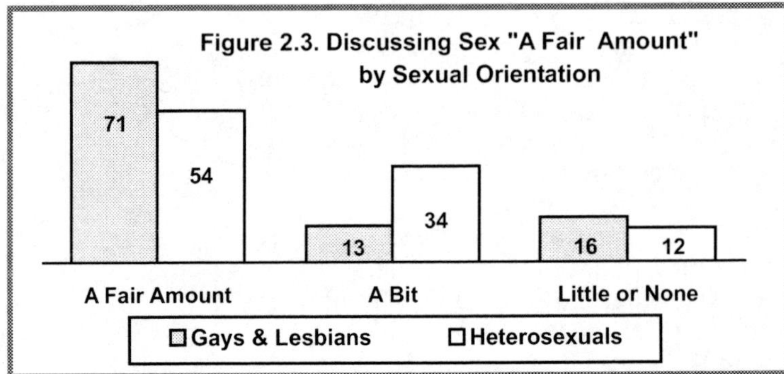

Sexual Attitudes

We probed sexual attitudes in two ways. First, we asked how Canadians view or have viewed their own children engaging in a variety of sexually related activities. Second, we asked how they view **people as a whole** engaging in some of those same activities.

In both instances **we attempted to differentiate between approval and acceptance**. We realize that parents, for example, may not approve of certain things, but nonetheless are willing to accept them. As some of our previous survey respondents have said about their sons and daughters' lifestyle decisions, "I might not like it — but what choice do I have?"

- *Premarital sex* is something that gains the approval and acceptance of more than 5 in 10 adults, providing their children are 18 or older. Close to another 4 in 10 say they disapprove but nonetheless are willing to accept their children's premarital sexual activities. More than half say that, while they disapprove or have disapproved of their offspring engaging in sex prior to 18, their response nonetheless is or was one of acceptance.

- In the case of *homosexuality*, less than three in ten people say they would approve or have approved of their children engaging in homosexual acts, but another three in ten say they would be accepting, despite their disapproval. However, if a child informed them that he or she was gay or lesbian, acceptance and approval would rise or has risen substantially. In such cases, close to 4 in 10 would be approving and accepting and another 4 in 10 would disapprove but accept the disclosure. Some 25% would be disapproving and not accepting — considerably fewer than the 45% who would take or have taken such a posture toward their children engaging in homosexual acts.

- *Cohabitation* receives the approval and acceptance of 5 in 10 people, while just over 3 in 10 say their reaction is one of disapproval but acceptance. In the case of their offspring *having children without being married*, the proportions are reversed — 5 in 10 disapprove but accept, and 3 in 10 approve and accept. The remaining 2 in 10 neither approve of nor accept such a situation.

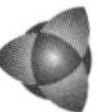

- One activity for which there is limited acceptance and even less approval is *sexual involvement outside of marriage*. Here only 3% indicate they would be or have been approving and accepting; about 75% say their response is both disapproval and non-acceptance.

Attitudes toward sexual activity have been changing over time. We asked our respondents whether or not sex "was pretty common among teenagers" in their high schools. No less than 74% of Gen-Xers said it was, compared to 41% of Baby-Boomers and 12% of Pre-Boomers.

Table 2.6. Attitudes Toward Childrens Sexual Behaviour

"How do you feel - or did you feel/or would you feel - about your children..."

	Approve & Accept	Disapprove But Accept	Disapprove & Do Not Accept	Totals
Engaging in premarital sex when they are 18 or older	53%	36	11	100
Engaging in premarital sex prior to age 18	17	54	29	100
Informing you that they are gay or lesbian	35	42	23	100
Engaging in homosexual acts	24	31	45	100
Living with a sexual partner without being married	53	35	12	100
Having children without being married	33	50	17	100
Having sexual relations with someone other than their spouse	3	23	74	100

Such generational differences in perceived behaviour are also readily apparent when we look at attitudes.

- Canadian adults *under the age of 35* are considerably *less likely to express disapproval and non-acceptance* of their children having premarital sex at any age, engaging in homosexual acts, learning their children are gay or lesbian, the arrival of grandchildren when their sons and daughters are not married, and having their children live together. About 7 to 8 in 10 draw the line at extramarital sex.

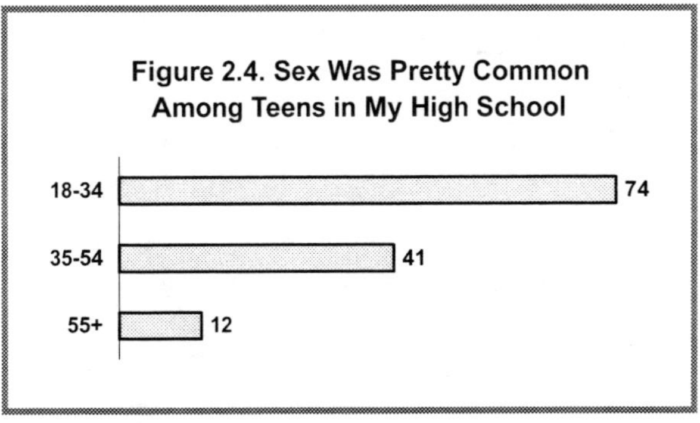

Figure 2.4. Sex Was Pretty Common Among Teens in My High School

- Attitudinal age differences are similar for females and males with two exceptions: young males are not as positive as females about people engaging in homosexual acts, and are not quite as negative about extramarital sex.

- For young adults who are actively involved in religious groups it's a different story. They are considerably more likely to disapprove and be non-accepting of all these activities. Nonetheless, only three kinds of activities receive a negative response from more than 50%: premarital sex prior to 18, homosexual acts and extramarital sex. Weekly-attending 18- to- 34-year-olds, for example, indicate more acceptance—if not approval—of premarital sex, a child disclosing she or he is gay, having children without being married, and cohabitation.

Table 2.7. Disapproval and Non-Acceptance of Children's Sexual Behaviour by Gender, Age, and Religious Service Attendance

"% Indicating they "Disapprove and Do Not Accept..."

	NAT	18-34	35-54	55+	18-34 Female	18-34 Male	18-34 Weekly+	18-34 <Weekly
Engaging in premarital sex prior to age 18	29%	19	28	40	18	20	57	11
Engaging in premarital sex when 18 or older	11	9	9	18	8	10	37	3
Engaging in homosexual acts	45	27	45	63	24	31	71	18
Informing you that they are gay or lesbian	22	12	23	32	12	13	29	9
Having children without being married	17	8	16	30	8	7	28	3
Living with partner without being married	12	9	10	17	8	10	37	3
Having sexual relations other than spouse	74	69	74	79	74	63	90	65

As might be expected, Canadian's are somewhat more likely to indicate approval and acceptance of various kinds of sexually related behaviours when their own children are not involved.

- The pattern is true for both premarital sex and homosexual activity.
- It also holds true for sex with someone other than one's marital or common-law partner, although the dominant response is still disapproval, whether one's offspring is involved or not.

Table 2.8. Attitudes Toward Ones Own Childrens Sexual Behaviour vs. Society as a Whole

	Approve & Accept	Disapprove But Accept	Disapprove & Do Not Accept	Totals
Sexual relations between an unmarried man and woman	**65%**	**25**	**10**	**100**
Own children engaging in premarital sex when 18 or older	53	36	11	100
Sexual relations between two people of the same sex	**33**	**29**	**38**	**100**
Own children Engaging in homosexual acts	24	31	45	100
Sexual relations with someone other than...				
Ones marital partner	**4**	**27**	**69**	**100**
Ones common -law partner	**4**	**29**	**67**	**100**
Own children having sexual relations other than with their spouse	3	23	74	100

Cohabitation

We posed a number of questions to help clarify the nature of cohabitation in Canadian life. First, we looked at attitudes:

- 45% of the respondents maintain that cohabiting before marriage *makes for better marriages.*

- 64% believe that cohabitation *does not involve the same commitment level* as marriage, while 43% feel it *doesn't involve the same level of sexual loyalty* as marriage.

- Over 6 in 10 say that cohabitation *tends to be pre-marital and post-marital* in nature, rather than an actual substitute for marriage.

- *Younger adults* are more likely than older adults to think cohabitation is associated with better marriages, involves commitment and loyalty, and does not tend only to be temporary.

- The views of *young females and males* tend to be very similar with two exceptions: males are far more likely than females to maintain that cohabitation: (1) does not match marriage's level of sexual loyalty and (2) is not usually a substitute for marriage.

- Young weekly *religious service attendees* consistently take a much more negative view of cohabitation that their non-weekly attending counterparts— again demonstrating that religion overrides age in influencing attitudes.

Table 2.9. Attitudes Toward Cohabitation by Age, Gender and Religious Service Attendance

"% Indicating they Strongly Agree or Agree"

	NAT	18-34	35-54	55+	18-34			
					Female	*Male*	*Weekly+*	*<Weekly*
People who live together first are more apt to have a good marriage	45%	64	43	30	63	66	21	73
Cohabitation does not involve the same level of commitment as marriage	64	55	65	73	53	57	79	50
Cohabitation does not involve the same level of sexual loyalty as marriage	43	31	41	58	21	41	53	26
Cohabitation tends to be something people do before or after marriage, but it is seldom a life-long substitute for marriage	61	54	58	72	47	62	73	50

That's what people *think*. Apart from their perceptions, what do people who are actually living together have to say about all this?

To begin with, **12% of Canadian adults say that they are currently cohabiting, led by Quebeckers at 22%**. The second highest figure is in British Columbia (13%), followed in order by the Prairies (8%), Ontario (7%), and the Atlantic provinces (4%).[8] **However, if we ask about cohabitation experiences over one's lifetime, a somewhat different picture emerges.**

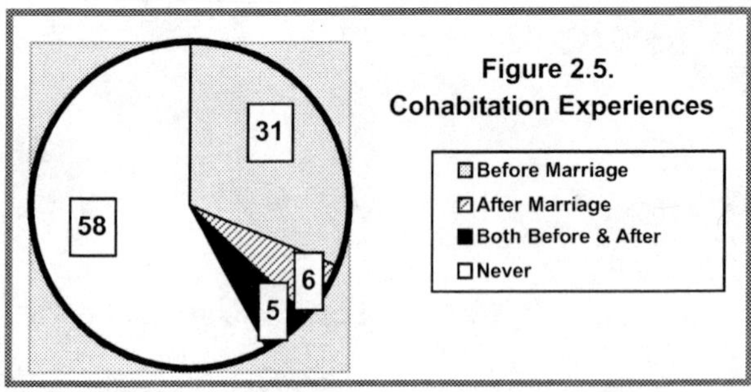

Figure 2.5. Cohabitation Experiences

- Over 4 in 10 Canadians report that they have lived with a "non-marital sexual partner."

- In 3 of the 4 cases, the cohabitation has been *pre-marital*; the remaining 1 in 4 instances have been *post-marital*.

- One in 20 people say that they have cohabited both *before and after* marriages.

- Contrary to the single snapshot data on marital status, the experience of cohabitation is actually highest for people who *currently live in B.C.*, followed by Quebec and the Prairies, then Ontario and then Atlantic Canada.

- One in 2 adults *under the age of 55* say they at some point lived with a sexual partner, as have 1 in four 4 people age 55 *and over.*

- Age, however, is not the only salient cohabitation determinant: among adults under 35, differences are evident between both *females* (54%) and *males* (40%) and between people *not highly involved in religious groups* (53%) and *those who are* (25%).

Table 2.10. Cohabitation by Select Variables

"Have you ever lived together with a non marital sexual partner"

	Yes Prior	**Yes** After	**Yes** Both	**No**	**Totals**
Nationally	31%	6	5	58	100
BC	41	4	7	48	100
Quebec	34	11	7	48	100
Prairies	30	4	3	63	100
Ontario	28	5	4	63	100
Atlantic	26	2	2	70	100
18-34	43	1	3	53	100
35-54	37	6	8	49	100
55+	12	9	3	76	100
18-34	43	1	3	53	100
Females	*48*	*2*	*4*	*46*	*100*
Males	*38*	*<1*	*2*	*60*	*100*
Less Weekly	*50*	*<1*	*3*	*47*	*100*
Weeklys	*16*	*4*	*5*	*75*	*100*

An examination of the current marital status and divorce/separation history of the 40% of Canadians who have cohabited at some point in their lives—804 people in our sample—**is revealing.**

- About 3 in 4 *eventually got married*—not necessarily to the individual or individuals with whom they had lived.[9]

- No less than 58% of those who have never married say that it is either *"very important"* (27%) or *"somewhat important"* (31%) *for them to marry* in their lifetimes.

- Of those who have never been married, 2 in 3 think they *will or may eventually marry*, including about 80% of those between the ages of 18 and 34.

- Cohabiting Canadians who have never married range from a high of 13% of the adult population in *Quebec*, 9% in *British Columbia*, 6% on the *Prairies*, and 4% in *Ontario*, to a low of 2% in the *Atlantic* region.

Table 2.11 Marital Status to date of Canadians Who Have Cohabited

EVENTUALLY MARRIED		**74%**
Have not divorced or separated	31	
Remarried after divorce or separation	6	
Divorced or separated	36	
Widowed (one-thrid divorced/separated)	1	
NEVER MARRIED		**26%**
18-34	17	
35-54	7	
55-plus	2	
TOTAL		**100**

Some facts about people who are currently cohabiting:

- Couples have been together for an *average* of five years; the range in our sample is from a month or so to 33 years.

- Roughly 93% of those cohabiting describe themselves as having "committed" relationships rather than "casual", with virtually the same percentage and the same people indicating that their partners view the relationship the same way (correlation coefficient of r = .850).

- The marital plans of "the current cohort" of cohabiting couples as a whole—versus only those who have never been married:

  - ✓ 39% say they expect to eventually marry their current partner
  - ✓ 5% indicate they expect to marry but are unsure who the person will be
  - ✓ 19% tell us that they "perhaps" eventually will marry
  - ✓ the remaining 37% say "no," they don't plan to marry—including the person who has been living common-law for 33 years.

- At this point, about 45% of cohabiting Quebeckers say they do not intend to get married. In contrast, people in similar situations in British Columbia, for example—despite their sizeable numbers—in the majority of cases maintain their cohabitation status is not life-long.[10]

Table 2.12. Marital Plans of People Currently Cohabiting

	NAT	Que	BC
WILL EVENTUALLY MARRY	**44%**	**31**	**57**
Current partner	39	31	41
Unsure who it will be	5	<1	16
PERHAPS WILL MARRY	**19**	**24**	**6**
NOT PLANNING TO MARRY	**37**	**45**	**37**
TOTAL	**100**	**100**	**100**

Summary Note

The terminology about Canadians' spending time with each other prior to marrying and cohabiting appears to have changed from an emphasis on "dating" to "going out" and "hanging out." Yet the inclination both to meet one another and spend time together in groups has changed little over time. The age when the majority of people have begun to "date" and "go out" has remained at around sixteen since at least the 1940s—with sixteen also the age that most people regard as ideal.

The two qualities that stand out as the most desirable in a partner are honesty and kindness. Other top-rated characteristics include respect, compatibility and humour. The importance of these characteristics differs little by either age or gender.

Most Canadians report they have learned about sexuality through friends and books. A secondary source of information has been the media and school courses, with a third level comprised of family members, led by mothers, followed by siblings, and then fathers. Smaller numbers of people also note the contributions of religious groups and partners/spouses. What stands out over time is not so much the change in the ranking of sex information sources as much as the increase in the extent to which almost all sources are seen as providing information. This seems to reflect the reality that the discourse on sexuality has become much more public in recent decades.

THE LONGER LOOK

Acceptance of Sexual Relations and Approval of Legal Abortion by Age Cohorts: 1975 and 2000*

	1975	2000
PREMARITAL RELATIONS		
Nationally	**68%**	**84**
18-34	90	93
35-54	65	89
55+	42	74
HOMOSEXUAL RELATIONS		
Nationally	**28**	**73**
18-34	42	75
35-54	25	64
55+	**12**	**42**
LEGAL ABORTION A POSSIBILITY...		
"If her own health is seriously endangered"		
Nationally	**94**	**94**
18-34	97	98
35-54	92	95
55+	93	90
"If she is married and doesn't want more children"		
Nationally	**45**	**52**
18-34	47	51
35-54	43	44
55+	45	48

* Sexual relations: % Indicating *"Not Wrong At All" or "Sometimes Wrong"* Versus "Always Wrong" or "Almost Always Wrong"; Legal abortion: % Indicating, "Yes," it should be possible.

Source: Reginald W. Bibby, Project Canada Survey Series.

Our survey probed sexual attitudes Canadians have or have had toward their own children engaging in sexual activities, versus people in general. We also tried to distinguish between approval and acceptance. Approval and acceptance are highest for premarital sex when their offspring are adults and when they are living common-law. Yet even in these two instances, the approval/acceptance levels barely exceed 50%. Parental attitudes tend to take the form of disapproval but acceptance in a number of instances, such as their children engaging in sex prior to eighteen, their children informing them they are gay or lesbian, and having children without being married. Disapproval and non-acceptance is the dominant response to their children engaging in homosexual acts and—in some 75% of cases—extramarital sex. Acceptance and approval tend to be inversely related to age. People are somewhat more likely to approve and accept various activities when their own children are not involved.

A widely accepted idea is that common-law relationships are becoming increasingly popular, especially in Quebec, signalling the demise of traditional marriage. Large numbers of survey respondents think that non-married people who cohabit lack commitment and sexual loyalty but this is not borne out. Further, an examination of over 800 people who have lived together shows that about 75% eventually married and many others expect to do so. Even in Quebec, most people who cohabit eventually marry. Current claims to the contrary warrant watching.

We turn now to marriage and what it means to Canadians.

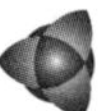

Reflections
How Canadians Think and Act Premaritally

It's widely believed that the sexual revolution of the1960s left a legacy of pervasive sexual permissiveness. During the past fifty years sex has “gone public” to an unprecedented extent in Canada, openly discussed and portrayed in any number of institutional and entertainment venues. Greater openness has been accompanied by more permissive attitudes and, presumably, by a higher incidence of sexual activity outside of marriage. The latter in turn is seen as contributing to an increasing number of couples opting for cohabitation over marriage. The alleged net result has been the decline in the perceived need for and popularity of conventional marriage.

These now taken-for-granted assumptions and claims about cultural change appear to be greatly exaggerated. In the early years of the twenty-first century, the average age at which Canadians begin to pursue romantic relationships has changed little from that of their grandparents. To be sure, attitudes toward premarital sex and homosexuality have become more liberal over the past five decades. But “becoming more liberal” should not be confused with the disappearance or even the erosion of sexual values and expectations.

It's true that about 90% of Canadians are willing to accept the reality of premarital sex among adults. But while about 65% say they actually approve of such behaviour, the approval level slips to around 55% when respondents are asked if they approve of premarital sex for their own children. And even fewer Canadians approve of sexual activity involving teenagers under the age of 18.

Further, only about one in three Canadians currently express both approval and acceptance of homosexual acts, while 40% say the neither approve of nor are willing to accept such behaviour. Although more than two-thirds of our respondents would be willing to accept that their child was gay, only one out of every four parents would approve. Some 25% of parents have told us that they would neither approve of nor find acceptable their child's homosexuality.

Lest anyone harbour illusions that Canada's sexual norms are a thing of the past, he or she only needs to look at the findings concerning extramarital sex. Less than 5% of people across the country approve of and accept such behaviour; conversely, 70% neither approve nor are willing to accept people having sex with someone other than their spouse. The remaining one in four Canadians say they disapprove of but would accept or tolerate the reality of extramarital relationships. These levels of disapproval are virtually unchanged since the 1970s. The sexual revolution clearly did not extend to endorsing or legitimizing extramarital sex.

Finally, the liberalizing of attitudes toward premarital sex has made marriage optional for growing numbers of people. However, they continue to be in the minority. Most individuals who cohabit either eventually marry their partners or someone else, or already have been married. To date, cohabitation has been, for most people, a premarital, intermarital or postmarital experience.

All of this points to some important changes but also to remarkable stability when it comes to the premarital attitudes and experiences of Canadians. The age at which dating begins has remained steady for at least fifty years. Attitudes toward heterosexual and homosexual relationships have become more open but most Canadians reject promiscuity. Cohabitation has become more common, but in most cases it is a complement to marriage rather than a substitute for it.

What has been happening premaritally in Canada is not as revolutionary as many people think. To quote a sage of old, “There are a few things new under the sun. But just a few.”[11]

Some Issues Raised by the Findings

1. The difference between what Canadians approve of sexually, versus what they are willing to accept, needs to be recognized and widely discussed.

2. To what extent do we, as a society, wish to promote that which we approve of as well as protect the rights of others to behave in ways that we accept without approval?

3. If most Canadians are willing to accept, if not approve of, homosexuality, is there a responsibility to educate parents about the possible consequences of rejecting their children on the basis of their sexual orientation?

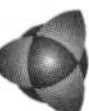

Marriage

The survey examined a range of questions relating to how people value marriage, including who marries and why, what people enjoy and don't enjoy about marriage, and their attitudes on a number of current issues.

People Who Marry

About 61% of respondents told us that they have been married once, while 7% acknowledged that they have been married more than once—1% three times or more. The remaining 32% have never married.

- About 9 in 10 Canadians who are married are *in their first marriages*.

- Obviously most of the people who describe themselves as *widowed* or *divorced/separated* have been formally married. The fact that some say they have not when we ask for marital details is a reminder that many people define "living together" and common-law marriages as marriages. The same blurriness is suggested by the fact that 1% who say they have never married also give us the year and ceremony details on their first "marriage." One young woman commented, "My first marriage was when I was young and it lasted only a month; I don't really count it."

- Obviously, having been married and being married more than once are both directly tied to *age*; differences by *gender* are negligible.

Table 3.1. Ever-Married Canadians

"Are you yourself married, or ***have you been married?"***

	Once	Two+	No	Totals
Nationally	**61%**	**7**	**32**	**100**
Married	88	11	1	100
Widowed	92	6	2	100
Div-Sep	84	9	7	100
Cohabiting	20	3	77	100
Never Mar	1	0	99	100
55+	79	12	9	100
35-54	70	9	21	100
18-34	30	<1	70	100
Males	61	8	31	100
Females	61	7	32	100
Atlantic	71	8	21	100
Prairies	64	7	29	100
Ontario	64	8	28	100
BC	56	9	35	100
Quebec	52	5	43	100

- The highest proportion of married adults is found in the *Atlantic region*, the lowest in *Quebec*. There is little difference by region in the inclination to remarry, although the tendency is slightly lower in Quebec than elsewhere.

As we saw in our examination of cohabitation, it is clear that, at minimum, many Canadians are postponing marriage.[12] An examination of the marital composition of young adults, 18 to 34 (using Project Canada data for 1975 and 1990 and our current 2003 survey) illustrates the magnitude of the changes in marital choices.

- These three surveys show the percentage of young adults who are married has plummeted from about 60% to 30%.

- There have been corresponding increases in the proportion of younger people who have never married and those who are cohabiting.

Table 3.2. Marital Composition of 18-34-year-olds: 1975, 1990 and 2003

	Married	Never Married	Divorced-Separated	Cohabitating	Totals
1975	61%	33	5	1	100
1990	48	36	3	13	100
2003	27	47	4	22	100

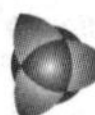

Cohabitation and delaying marriage—in part because of changing sexual mores—are frequently seen as associated with the decline in the importance of organized religion. A related, widely-held assumption is that Canadians who marry increasingly opt for civil rather than religious wedding ceremonies.

- The survey found that 87% of *first marriages* have been accompanied by religious ceremonies. The drop has come with *second marriages*; yet even here, a slight majority of 56% have been religious in nature.[13] As for *the future*, 63% of those who say they plan to marry say they want to have a religious ceremony. There is good reason to believe that may be a modest projection, given that many of these respondents are younger and at a life cycle point when religious involvement is typically fairly low. Clearly the demand for religious rites of passage remains very high.

- The religious ceremony pattern of "high for first, lower for second" holds across *age, gender* and *regional* categories. The inclination to prefer a religious ceremony to a civil one also differs little by age or gender.

- *Regionally*, religious wedding ceremonies in recent decades have been the least common in British Columbia (76%). What's more, two-thirds of the people on the west coast who plan to marry indicate they will be looking in civil directions—including a few in the sample who are looking for same-sex blessings. To the extent that Quebeckers marry, the vast majority of their first-time marriages have been religious—usually Catholic. Furthermore, marriage-minded people in Quebec report that they plan to look to the church in the future.

Table 3.3. Religious vs. Civil Ceremonies

% Indicating a Religious Ceremony

	First	Second	Future
National	**87%**	**56**	**63**
55+	93	***	***
35-54	83	48	52
18-34	82	64	66
Males	88	60	60
Females	85	51	66
Atlantic	93	67*	***
Quebec	90	50*	80
Ontario	88	62*	66
Prairies	84	56*	60
BC	76	41*	33

* N's small and percentages unstable; included for heuristic purposes.

Asked if there is an *ideal* age for people who want to marry to do so, Canadians are evenly divided. There is considerable consensus among those who think there is an ideal age for marriage.

- *Nationally*, the average (mean) ideal age that is cited for men is 26.3, women about a year and a half younger at 24.9.

- *Differences* by *age* are fairly small but consistent: younger adults tend to see the ideal ages as somewhat higher than older adults.

- The average age of marriage for people in the sample was 25.0—25.9 for men, and 24.3 for women; median ages were 25 and 23 respectively, with very little difference between the three age cohorts for both women and men.[14]

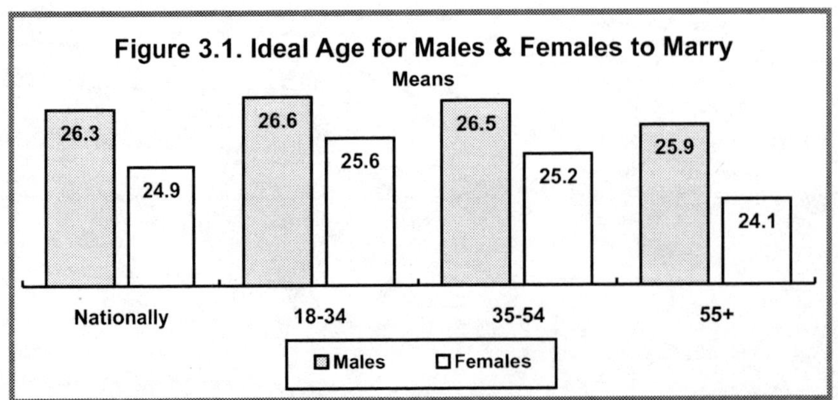

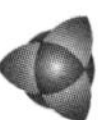

The Importance of Marrying

We asked respondents, *"How important would you say it was—or is—for you to get married in your lifetime?"*

- Eighty per cent said it was/is "very important" (47%) or "somewhat important" (33%).
- The remaining 20% either said that marrying was/is "not very important" (12%) or "not important at all" (8%) to them.
- Because high proportions of people see being married as important suggests that we cannot assume that a delay in marrying means people have given up on marriage.

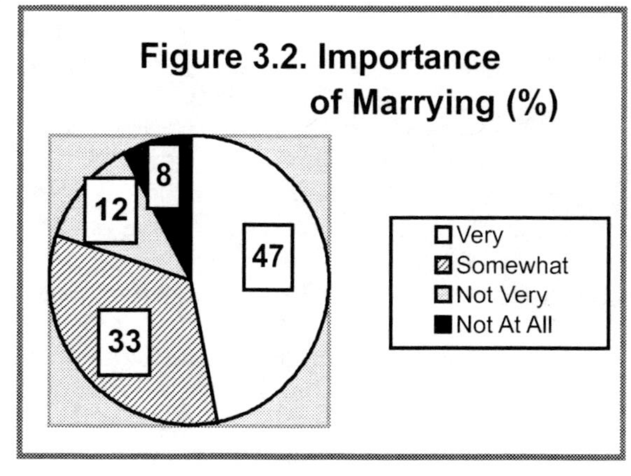

The importance placed on getting married is fairly similar across the country, with one well-documented exception: Quebec. Consistent with other research findings documenting the devaluing of traditional marriage in Quebec in the post 1960s, Quebeckers are considerably less likely to indicate it has been or is important for them to marry at some point.

Outside Quebec, the inclination for people to see getting married as important differs little by such variables as gender, age, education or religious service attendance. Modest differences are limited primarily to males (87%) versus females (79%), and weekly service attendees (92%) versus people who attend less often or not at all (80%).

Table 3.4. Importance of Marrying by Region

% Indicating Very Important or Somewhat Important

Nationally	**80%**
Atlantic	86
Prairies	85
Ontario	83
BC	80
Quebec	67

In Quebec, 2 in 3 people do indicate that getting married is or has been important to them. There are limited differences by gender and education. However, two important variations stand out.

- Adults 18-34 and 35-54 (about 60% each) differ fairly dramatically from those 55 and over (85%) in their view of the importance of marriage. Very significantly, almost all of those younger adults were born after 1950, and have felt the transforming effects of the Quiet Revolution.
- Of those Quebeckers who *attend services regularly*, their inclination to want to marry is about the same as weekly attendees in the rest of the country.

Those who indicated that getting married was or is important to them were then asked to what extent a number of factors were or are important to them *"in choosing to marry versus, for example, living together with your partner without being married?"* An opportunity was also given to cite any one additional factor that had not been listed.

Three reasons stand out. The first is the feeling that *marriage signifies commitment* (93%), the second is moral values (85%), and the third is the *belief that children should have married parents* (77%).

- These three factors are ranked the same by women and men, as well as by Gen-Xers, Boomers and Pre-Boomers, although the levels of endorsement increase with age.

- Quebec residents are about as likely to see commitment and moral value factors as important, but are less inclined (63%) to hold the same view as people elsewhere (81%) about believing children should have married parents.

Somewhat smaller majorities of about 6 in 10 Canadians say that marriage was or is "just the *natural thing* to do," that *financial security* is an important consideration, and that *religious beliefs* were or are a motivating factor. Relatively small numbers say that pressure from either family or friends was or is a major influence in wanting to marry.

- Quebeckers are less likely than people elsewhere to see financial security and social pressure as important factors.

- *Women and men* differ little in their relative endorsement of all five of these reasons for marrying; however, age continues to be directly related to a greater endorsement of everything, with the exception of pressure from family and friends.

Table 3.5. Importance of Marrying by Select Variables

" % Indicating Very Important or Somewhat Important"

	NAT	Quebec	Rest of Canada
ALL	**80%**	**67**	**83**
Married	92	85	94
Widowed	85	***	82
Divorced-Sep	76	80	75
Never Married	63	52	67
Cohabiting	51	31	68
Males	82	65	87
Females	77	69	79
55+	87	85	87
35-54	75	59	80
18-34	78	61	84
Univ Grads	79	69	82
Tech-Bus	81	61	87
HS or Less	80	69	83
Weeklys	92	93	92
Less Weekly	75	61	80

Table 3.6. Reasons for Wanting to Marry

"% Indicating Very Important or Somewhat Important"

	Nationally	ROC	Quebec	Women	Men	18-34	35-54	55+
Feeling that marriage signifies commitment	93%	94	90	92	93	90	92	98
Moral values	85	86	82	85	86	77	86	93
Belief children should have married parents	77	81	63	76	77	64	77	89
It was/is the natural thing to do	66	65	69	64	67	55	65	77
Financial security	60	64	46	64	56	54	59	68
Religious beliefs	59	59	59	62	57	51	55	73
Pressure from family	27	29	19	29	25	27	28	27
Pressure from friends	13	16	3	16	11	16	12	14

Marriage—The Good and The Bad

We asked married and previously married survey participants to list "one thing" they like about marriage. The level of consensus was high among five major factors cited by 2 in 3 people. They were:

- *the relationship*, complete with characteristics such as companionship, love and support;
- a sense of *security* that also provides stability;
- the characteristics of their *partner*, including such traits as commitment, trust and reliability;
- the sense of *family* they experience, versus being individuals only;
- and *children* — valuing them and feeling the marriage adds to their children's lives.

Table 3.7. The Top Five Things People Like About Marriage

1. The Relationship	35%
2. Sense of Security	15
3. Partners Traits	9
4. Sense of Family	5
5. Children	2

We also probed the negative side of marriage, asking those who are married or were married to list "one source of tension." Here the list was more varied, lending itself to "a top ten" list.

- The number one source of tension cited was *finances* (36%).
- Following a distant second but still mentioned almost twice as often as anything else—was *children* (9%). Tension here is frequently associated with different views on how children should be raised and/or disciplined.
- An additional eight issues—most of which receive considerable media attention—round out the top sources of tension: *household tasks, communication, personal traits* (such as moodiness and habits), *conflict, personal differences, anxiety about the relationship, careers,* and *extended family members* including in-laws.

Table 3.8. The Top Ten Things People Say Add Tension to Marriage

1. Finances	36%
2. Children	9
3. Sharing Household Duties	5
4. Lack of Communication	5
5. Personal Traits	5
6. Conflict	5
7. Personal Differences	4
8. Anxiety About Relationship	4
9. Careers	3
10. Extended Family Members	3

"One thing I like about marriage...." and "One source of Tension..."
Some Response Examples

ONE THING I LIKE
...my partner...you are never lonely...security...feeling special for someone...my spouse is my best friend...stability...two people who complete each other...compatibility...lifelong friendship and support...being together...the possibility of building together...mutual effort...comfort...I am trusted and respected...loyalty being able to share...fidelity...sharing life together...raising our children together ...intimacy...happiness...having someone there for me...lovingness...companionship...working together...knowing I am accepted for myself...sex...not being alone...nothing...togetherness...family life...lifestyle...partnership ...life bond...

ONE SOURCE OF TENSION
...value differences...money...raising children...nagging...illness...no time for each other...fatigue...attempts to dominate...finances ...I'm working, he's retired...lack of confidence...occasional selfishness...financial burden...mood swings...stepchildren ...different goals ...no sex...misunderstandings...income...lack of help with responsibilities...jealousy...more than just my view to contend with... monotony...squabbles...gender ideas...disrespect...inflexibility...sharing housework...disapproval...lack of compromise...inability to have children...loneliness...smoking...feeling tied-down...kids...drinking...disagreements...equality...religion...bills... Lifestyle differences... Time-management...lack of support...fidelity...spending money on the home...lack of love...

Some Attitudes Concerning Marriage

We posed a number of questions about marriage to further our understanding about what Canadians want, versus what they find themselves having to adapt to — what they value versus where they find themselves.

For example, **in the face of widespread divorce, have Canadians ceased to believe in the possibility of the permanence of marriage?** The example in this case is a decisive "No."

- A near-unanimous 95% of people across the country maintain that, ideally at least, marriage should last a lifetime.

- Some 9 in 10 say that they expect their own marriages and relationships "to last the rest of my life."

- Those dreams are not new: more than 8 in 10 said that, as teenagers they "expected to stay with the same partner for life." Some 9 in 10 Canadian teenagers have been expressing that same idea since at least the early-1990s.[15]

We have just seen that how to deal with children and the sharing of household duties are sources of tension for many married couples. If that's the case, the overwhelming majority would seem to be receptive to having something done about it.

- Virtually everyone agrees that parents need to take equal responsibility for raising their kids. There is no other single item in the questionnaire that receives the endorsement of more married people.

- What's more, just about as many say that couples should share household duties equally.

Despite the high divorce rate and despite all the tension that is acknowledged, married couples – at least while they still are together – are very positive about their marriages.

- Just about everyone says they are either "very happy" or "pretty happy" with their marital relationships.

- 95% say that, "If I were doing it all again, I would marry."

Table 3.9. Attitudes Toward Marriage Length and Roles
"% Indicating they Strongly Agree or Agree"

	NAT	Que	ROC
Lasting Marriages			
Ideally, marriage should last a lifetime	95%	93	96
I expect my marriage/relationship to last the rest of my life	91	90	92
As a teenager, I expected to stay with the same partner for life	82	87	80
Marital Roles			
Parents need to take equal responsibility for raising children	99	99	99
Couples should share household duties equally	94	97	93
Marital Satisfaction			
Describe marriage as "very happy" or "pretty happy"	97	98	96
Married or Widowed: If I were doing it all again, I would marry	95	93	95

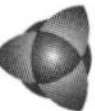

How do Canadians stand on some controversial marriage matters? We asked for participants' thoughts on some tough topics including same-sex rights and their experience with family violence. We also checked out their marital tolerance zones by getting their response to a fairly radical possibility.

We found that *just over half* the country agrees that governments need to give high priority to making sure **same-sex families** receive the **same benefits** as other Canadian families. We also found that *just under half the country* feels that **same-sex couples** should be **allowed to marry.**[16]

- In both instances, gays and lesbians receive somewhat greater support from people in *Quebec, younger adults*, *females*, and people who are *not actively involved* in religious groups.

- Opposition from people who are active in religious services is more pronounced in the case of marriage (79%) than in the receiving of benefits (63%).

Violence toward partners, according to our survey participants, is fairly common. Just under 1 in 2 people say that they *"have had some close friends who have experienced spousal violence."* [17]

- Such reports are slightly more common outside Quebec, but differ little by age.

- Younger adults are just as likely to report such a reality, regardless of gender or religious service attendance.

We saw earlier that Canadians, young and old, have some "near absolutes," drawing a sexual acceptance and approval line for extramarital sex.

- The survey found another such line is drawn in the case of marital structure: *4% say that they "approve and accept" the idea of "people being allowed to have more than one marital partner at a time."*

- Another 16% indicate they would disapprove but be willing to accept such a situation.[18]

Table 3.10. Attitudes Toward Additional Marriage Issues by Region, Age, Gender and Religious Service Attendance

% Indicating they "Strongly Agree" or "Agree"

	NAT	Que	ROC	18-34	35-54	55+	18-34 Female	18-34 Male	Weekly+	<Wkly
Same-Sex Rights										
Governments need to give high priority ensure same-sex families receive same benefits as other families	52	58	49	69	52	34	72	65	37	76
Same-sex couples should be allowed to marry	46	50	44	64	47	24	66	62	21	74
Violence										
Some close friends: experienced spousal violence	44	39	46	42	45	46	44	40	42	43
Multiple Partners: Approve & Accept										
Should be allowed have >1 marital partner at a time	4	6	4	4	6	2	3	5	1	5

A Gratification Comparison: Marriage and Cohabitation

According to our survey, over 80% of the couples who currently are living together are married while just under 20% are not. The following facts summarize our findings.

- Some 66% of Canadians who are cohabiting say that "I just don't see any need to marry versus live with someone." That view is held by 38% of never-married individuals who are not living with a partner.

- Still, 45% of those people who are cohabiting say they plan to marry, and 32% rule marriage out altogether; one-quarter of people in this latter category were previously married.

- The 45% figure shouldn't be surprising, given that 51% of those cohabiting acknowledge that it is or has been important for them to get married in their lifetimes. That level compares to 63% for those who have never married and are not cohabiting.

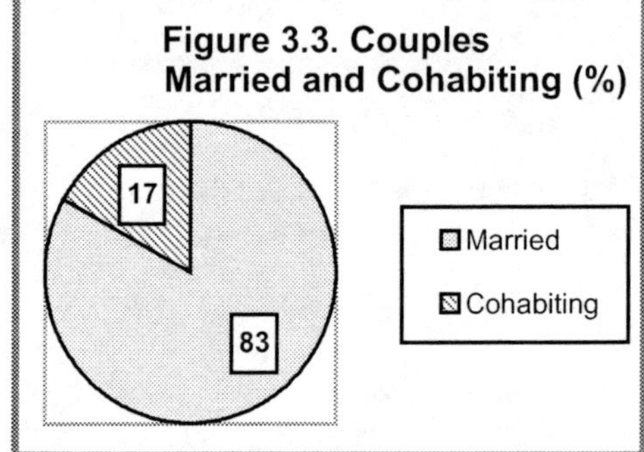

Figure 3.3. Couples Married and Cohabiting (%)

- The two areas of the country where cohabitation have been particularly prevalent are British Columbia and, to a greater extent, Quebec. In BC, there are signs that cohabitation is largely temporary; in Quebec, there are signs it could increasingly become an alternative to formal marriage.

What is important from the standpoint of quality of life is to take note of the contribution these alternate forms of family life are making to Canadians. We will return to this question throughout the analysis of the survey results.

At this point, we will take a preliminary look at the quality of life implications of marital and cohabitation choices. In the survey, we asked participants to indicate, on balance, *"how much enjoyment and how much strain"* they experience or have experienced with their *"marriage or relationship"*. Five possible combinations were posed, as indicated in Table 3.11.

Keep in mind that the results reported are not objective facts, but rather the subjective perceptions Canadians have of the enjoyment and strain they experience in their relationships.

Table 3.11. Self-Reported Experiences With Marriage and Cohabitation by Region, Gender, and Age

	Nationally		Quebec		ROC		Men		Women		18-34		35-54		55+	
	Marriage	Cohab	Mar	Co	Mar	Co	Mar	Co	Mar	Co	Mar	Co	Mar	Co	Mar	Co
Lots of enjoyment, very little strain	49%	35	42	30	50	40	53	38	43	34	53	40	46	30	51	35
Quite a bit of enjoyment, very little strain	34	34	45	38	32	30	35	28	34	37	32	32	34	36	35	35
Quite a bit of enjoyment, quite a bit of strain	15	26	11	27	16	25	10	29	21	24	14	28	18	23	11	20
Not very much enjoyment, very little strain	1	3	1	2	1	3	1	3	1	3	0	0	<1	5	2	5
Not very much enjoyment, quite a bit of strain	1	2	1	3	1	2	1	2	1	2	1	0	2	6	1	5
TOTALS	100%	100	← 100% →													

What the analysis reveals is a consistent tendency for people who are married to claim to experience higher levels of enjoyment and less strain that individuals who are cohabiting.

- For example, 49% of Canadians who are married say they are experiencing "lots of enjoyment and very little strain," compared to 35% of those who are living with a partner but are not married.

- Conversely, 26% of those cohabiting say their relationships are the source of "quite a bit of enjoyment and quite a bit of strain"—a claim made by 15% of married individuals.

Both married and unmarried couples clearly experience enjoyment and strain. However, **what is striking is that the modest differences in enjoyment versus strain are consistent across the array of variables examined**—outside and inside Quebec, among both women and men, or among adults regardless of generation.[19]

This could be an important finding with significant implications but it needs to be examined in greater detail with more care.

Table 3.12.
The Top Five Keys to a Happy and Lasting Relationship

1. Honesty	23%
2. Communication	20
3. Love	12
4. Patience	10
5. Respect	8

We asked Canadians, "What do you think is ***the key*** *to a happy and lasting relationship. This is what they had to say.*

"What do you think is THE KEY to a happy and lasting relationship?"
Some Response Examples

...give-and-take...love...confidence in each other...understanding...compatibility...honesty... forgetting self...take care of your partner...being good friends...willingness to work things out... allowing your partner freedom...forgiveness...stability...doing things together...common sense... caring...trust...each person giving 100%...acceptance...two forgiving people...communication of feelings...100% commitment to the relationship...trust...being flexible...acceptance of each other's beliefs and goals...sharing ideas...there are none...equality...honouring the vows taken...respect ...the ability to compromise...common interests... faithfulness...patience...mutual respect... communication all the time...kindness...willingness to work on things with a flexible attitude... dealing with things rather than getting angry...love and enough money...telling the truth...fidelity... being soul-mates...dependability...daily loving and caring...consideration of partner...listening... Respect for another's feelings...frankness...not controlling one another...passion...

THE LONGER LOOK

Approval of Intergroup Marriage: 1975-2000

	1975	1980	1985	1990	1995	2000
Whites and Natives	73%	81	83	84	84	91
Whites and Asians	64	75	78	82	84	90
Whites and East Indians/Pakistanis	56	66	72	76	81	87
Whites and Blacks	55	64	72	78	81	88

As of 2003, Canadians reporting interracial marriages & relationships: 4.0%.
By age: 18 to 34 - 7.3%, 35 to 54 - 3.4%, 55 & over - 2.7%.

Sources: Reginald W. Bibby, Project Canada Survey Series & Future Families Project.

Summary Note

The survey findings corroborate what we know intuitively—that the vast majority of adult Canadians either have been married or plan to marry. They also show that in the past three decades there has been a growing tendency for younger adults to at minimum postpone marriage and, to some extent, especially in Quebec, see cohabitation as an alternative to traditional marriage.

The findings also document the ongoing importance of marriage for the majority of Canadians. Some 80% of adults maintain that it has been or is important for them to marry in their lifetimes—including 60% of Quebec adults between the ages of 18 and 54. A majority of people across the country are still looking to religious groups for marriage ceremonies, particularly in the case of first marriages. This inclination is particularly pronounced in Quebec among people (primarily Roman Catholics) who anticipate getting married.

The three primary reasons Canadians say they want to marry is because they believe marriage signifies commitment, reflects their moral values and because they think children should have married parents. On the positive side, they say that marriage provides them with a unique relationship, security, positive partner traits, and a sense of family, complete with children. On the negative side, they acknowledge that marriage is not without strain on issues that include finances, raising children, household duties and communication. On balance, Canadians immensely value their relationships and aspire to overcome their sources of strain and have life-long marriages.

Despite the value they place on marriage, most are reluctant to be critical of other family arrangements. About half favour gays and lesbians having the right to marry, as well as to experience the same benefits as heterosexual families. However, not everything is okay: people are not about to recognize something like having several husbands or wives.

The emergence of cohabitation as a possible alternative to marriage—notably in Quebec—is an important development that needs to be much better understood, including some of the quality of life correlates. Our preliminary start in that direction will continue in our examination of children and parenting.

Reflections
How Canadians Feel About Marriage

During the 1970s considerable attention was given to the idea that marriage, as we have traditionally understood it, might soon become a thing of the past. Sexual liberation appeared to negate the once taken-for-granted assumption that legitimate sexual relations occurred only within marriage. There was even, for a relatively short period of time, talk of "open marriage" and "swinging" as alternatives to conventional marriage. Academics debated whether marriage specifically and family life more generally were experiencing "disorganization" or simply "reorganization."

Much of this preoccupation has proven to be unwarranted and, for the most part, the debates unnecessary. In the early years of this new century, marriage— traditional-style— continues to be solidly embraced by Canadians. Some eight in ten people have felt or feel that it's important for they themselves to marry during their lifetimes.

What's more, contrary to widespread conjecture, most first weddings still tend to be religious in nature, carried out by ministers, priests, rabbis, and other religious figures. The inclination to opt for a civil ceremony becomes more pronounced with second weddings; but even here, religious ceremonies outnumber their civil counterparts.

Yet, couples are aware marriage has its "ups and downs." In their own marriages, Canadians say that the major plus of marriage is the relationship itself; the major source of tension is finances. Still, on balance, no less than 97% describe their marriages as "very happy" or "pretty happy." Very few regret marrying: 95% say if they were to do it all again, they would marry. What's more, 95% continue to think that ideally marriage should last a lifetime and no less than 90% say that they personally expect to stay with their current partner for life. Those are pretty impressive endorsements of marriage.

Why do people continue to marry? Primarily, they say, because they feel that marriage signifies commitment. Other important reasons for many include moral values and the belief that children should have married parents. About two in three say that marriage is important to them simply because it seems like "the natural thing to do."

It's true that younger adults wait longer before marrying than did their parents and grandparents; but postponing the game is quite different from cancelling it. When asked pointedly, most unmarried younger adults say they intend to marry in the future. Our national surveys of teenagers have documented the same widespread intentions.

The important exception in all this is Quebec. Quebeckers who place importance on marriage and plan to marry continue to be in the majority. And those who when people plan to marry invariably want a religious ceremony. But the pro-marriage majority in Quebec is smaller than in the rest of the country. Whether or not Quebeckers are, as some have suggested, paving the way for similar attitudinal and behavioural changes in the rest of the country remains to be seen. A key factor in Quebec would seem to be the extent to which Quebeckers, most of whom still identify themselves as Roman Catholics, become more involved in the church. Current patterns suggest that, in the immediate future at least, to the extent people are involved in the Church, the tendency to embrace marriage can be expected to increase; conversely, the inclination to marry can be expected to decline with declining participation.

While most Canadians value marriage as it has been traditionally understood, they also seem to be flexible and adaptable. A slight majority feel that gay and lesbian couples, for example, should know the same benefits as other couples. Close to one in two also feel that such couples should be allowed to marry. However, Canadians are reluctant to accept variations on the traditional notion of marriage. Multiple marital partners are opposed by 96% of the population making polygamy, along with extramarital sex, one of the two near-absolute family "no-no's" in the minds of people across the country.

These findings show clearly that, despite all the earlier prognostications—complete with the hand-wringing of many and the enthusiasm of some—marriage remains solidly entrenched in Canada.

Some Issues Raised by the Findings

1. What can be done to help Canadians to sustain and strengthen marriages which they entered with the hope and expectation of a life-long commitment?

2. How can strong marriages be encouraged without such support leading to disparaging attitudes and policies toward other unions?

3. Is religion still a key institutional player in the widespread Canadian endorsement of marriage?

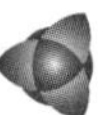

Children, Hopes and Values

In exploring what Canadians want from family life, the survey looked at "the real and ideal" concerning children and their parents. Themes included who is having children and why, what people want for their children, the kinds of people parents hope their children will become, and some child-rearing issues, including care of children and balancing employment and parenting. It also was important to get some up-to-date information on the relationship between children and parents as both get older. This section and section five focus on what we found.

People Who Have Children

Close to 70% of the people in our sample indicated that they have children—down from what 77% of our Project Canada sample reported in 1975.[20] The average number of children now being reported is 2.4, versus 2.9 in the mid-1970s.[21]

- About 45% of Canadians have either one or two children, a claim made by just under 40% in 1975.
- Over 20% have three or four children, compared to more than 25% in the 1970s.
- Just 3% today say they have five or more children, versus 12% in 1975.

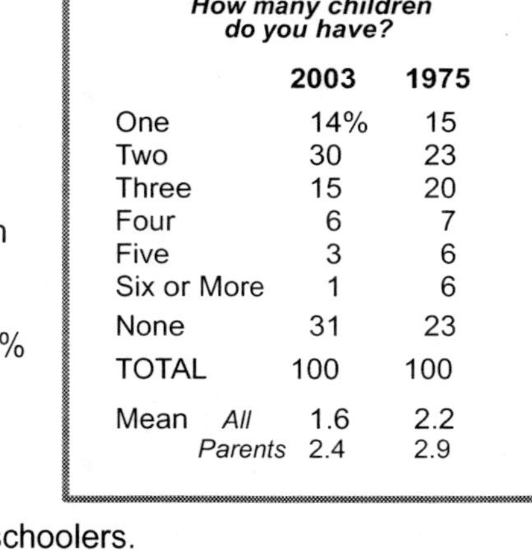

Table 4.1. Adults With Children: 1975-2003
How many children do you have?

	2003	1975
One	14%	15
Two	30	23
Three	15	20
Four	6	7
Five	3	6
Six or More	1	6
None	31	23
TOTAL	100	100
Mean *All*	1.6	2.2
Parents	2.4	2.9

"Children" obviously vary considerably in age.

- Just over 1 in 10 Canadian adults have children who are preschoolers.
- A slightly larger proportion has "kids" who are between the ages of 6 and 12.
- Almost 2 in 10 have teenagers.
- The children of another 4 in 10 are 20 or older. About 10% of these people say they have one or more such children currently living at home.

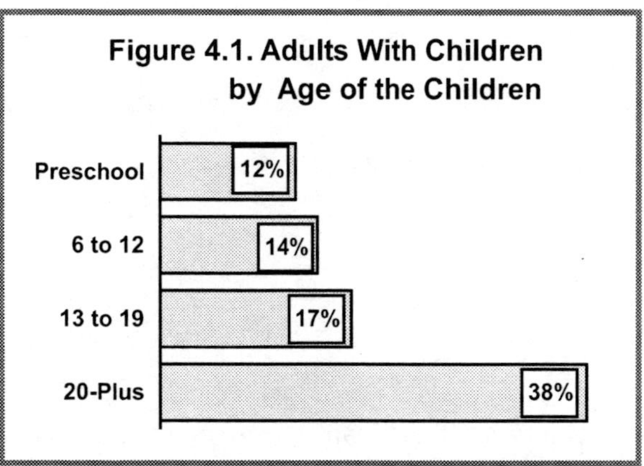

Figure 4.1. Adults With Children by Age of the Children

Having children or not having them is associated fairly predictably with such variables as marital status, age, gender and region.

- Reflecting smaller family sizes over time, Canadians who are *widowed* or *over the age of 55* report having more children than others.

- As we might expect, people *cohabiting* who have been married indicate they have more children on average (1.9) than those *cohabiting* who have never been married (.7).

- *Regionally*, the average number of children ranges from 1.9 per adult in the Atlantic region to 1.5 per adult in B.C.

- There is no significant difference in the number of children reported by *women* and *men*.

Table 4.2. Canadians With Children

"How many children do you have?"

	One	Two	Three+	None	Totals	Mean
Nationally	**14%**	**30**	**25**	**31**	**100**	**1.6**
Married	14	43	32	11	100	2.2
Widowed	14	26	47	13	100	2.5
Div-Sep	27	26	33	14	100	2.0
Cohabiting	17	20	14	49	100	1.1
Prev Mar	19	31	29	21	100	1.9
Never Mar	16	17	8	59	100	.7
Never Mar	5	2	<1	92	100	.1
55+	12	31	47	10	100	2.5
35-54	16	42	24	18	100	1.8
18-34	12	13	4	71	100	.5
Females	16	30	25	29	100	1.7
Males	12	30	24	34	100	1.6
Atlantic	14	34	28	24	100	1.9
Prairies	12	29	27	32	100	1.7
Ontario	13	30	26	31	100	1.6
Quebec	18	32	21	29	100	1.6
BC	9	29	23	39	100	1.5

We asked people who have had children or who want to have children what influenced or will influence the number of children they had or plan to have. Ten possible factors were listed, with respondents given the opportunity to cite any other key factor.

- The *number one* determinant cited by almost 8 in 10 respondents is the *strength of the relationship* they had or have with their partner.

- More than 6 in 10 said their *finances*, *their health*, and the feeling that *the current number was or is enough* were or are major determinants of family size.

- About 5 in 10 noted what they *could handle emotionally* and their *age* as key factors.

- Approximately 3 in 10 indicated that such diverse factors as two-family careers, infertility, and city or community where they are or will be living did or will influence how many children they have.

- Just 2 in 10 felt the issue is one that was or will be resolved by *chance*.

The inclination to cite these various determinants affecting one's number of children varies little between either *Quebec and the rest of Canada*, and *women and men*—although women are somewhat more likely than men to indicate that health and what they can handle emotionally are salient factors.

- The biggest differences are *age* differences: Gen-Xers are more likely than Boomers or Pre-Boomers to emphasize the importance of almost all factors.

- In doing so, they appear to be expressing a sense that they have greater control than their older counterparts did over how many children they will have. Significantly, they are less likely to say the final number will depend on either "feeling the current number is enough" or "chance".

- In large part, these age differences are associated with whether or not respondents already have children, versus plan to have them. Here we have an interesting peek at what many older people recall *were* key factors, versus what younger adults without children ideally think *should* be key factors. We can safely assume that the ideal will frequently give way to the real, as children arrive – or don't.

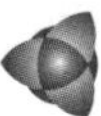

Table 4.3. Determinants of the Number of One's Children

"To what extent did/do these factors influence the number of children you had or plan to have?"

% Indicating "Very Important" or "Somewhat Important"

	Nationally	ROC	Quebec	Women	Men	18-34	35-54	55+	Have Children	No Children
Strength of my relationship	79%	79	81	78	81	86	77	76	75	92
Your finances	64	64	63	63	64	81	58	52	55	85
Your health	64	64	64	69	59	78	59	56	57	81
Feeling the current no. is enough	62	63	58	63	61	57	63	66	65	51
What could handle emotionally	51	53	45	57	44	65	48	40	43	70
Your age	47	48	42	51	43	55	45	41	40	64
Two-career family considerations	33	33	31	34	31	49	29	20	26	52
Infertility	31	32	28	32	31	44	26	25	21	55
City/community where live	28	29	27	28	28	43	22	22	22	44
Chance	21	21	19	25	16	18	19	26	21	18

This leads us to an important survey finding. **We asked Canadians**, ***"How many of your children would you say were actually 'planned?"***

- Nationally, 66% said that *all* of their children were planned—with the claim somewhat more common among men (70%) than women (63%). **This means that 1 in 3 adults with children acknowledge that at least one or more of their children were not planned. That translates into a lot of people!**

- There seems to be a pattern: *people who have had two children* are more likely than other parents to say that their two offspring were planned. Presumably, many with *one child* received a surprise. To the extent that Canadians have had *three or more children*, fewer and fewer, they report, were all planned—50% in the case of three children, 42% in the case of four, and 35% in situations where couples have had five or more children. In fact, when the number of children is more than five, approximately one in four parents—all over the age of 55—acknowledge that *none* were planned.

- *Age-wise*, so far, only 17% of adults under 35 say that all their children were planned, compared to 27% of those 35 to 54, and 21% of adults 55 and older. It remains to be seen the extent to which family planning intentions among Gen-Xers and younger Baby Boomers are realized.

Figure 4.2. Percentage of Their Children Parents Say "Were Actually Planned"

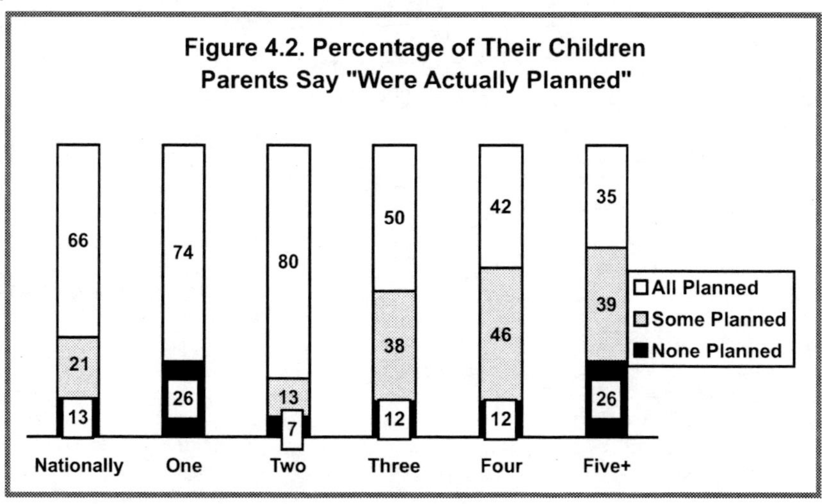

The Importance of Having Children

How central to life is being a parent? To probe the answer, we asked, ***"How important would you say it was— or is— for you yourself to have children in your lifetime?"***

- Nearly 9 in 10 replied, "Very" (61%) or "Somewhat Important" (26%).

- The remaining 1 in 10 said that having children was/is "not very important" (9%) or "not important at all" (4%) to them.

- Perhaps surprising to some readers, Quebeckers lead the country in saying they want to have children. They just don't plan to have as many as most people elsewhere. Our Project Teen Canada national survey in 2000, for example, found that 93% of Quebec youth 15 to 19 expect to have children. However, 68% said they plan to limit the number to one or two, compared to the intentions of 56% of young people elsewhere.

- The importance of having children is slightly higher among *women*, *older adults*, people who have *not graduated from university*, and *weekly religious service attendees* than others.

- The importance placed on having children is considerably higher among people who have had children versus those who have not.

Table 4.4. The Importance of Having Children by Select Variables

"How important was or is it for you yourself to have children in your life?

% Indicating "Very Important" or "Fairly Important"

	Very NB	Fairly NB	Not NB*	Totals
Nationally	**61%**	**26**	**13**	**100**
Quebec	68	23	9	100
Atlantic	67	17	16	100
Prairies	63	27	10	100
Ontario	60	27	13	100
BC	50	29	21	100
Women	65	22	13	100
Men	57	30	13	100
55+	71	19	10	100
35-54	61	24	15	100
18-34	53	33	14	100
Some PS	67	21	12	100
HS or Less	65	24	11	100
Univ Grads	55	29	16	100
Weeklys	69	22	9	100
Less Weekly	59	27	14	100
Have Children	75	21	4	100
Do not have children	34	32	34	100

"Not very important' or "Not important at all."

We asked people who indicated that they chose to not have children and those who do not intend to have children if there was or is one main reason for their decision. The question was open-ended.[22]

- The most frequently cited factors were *not being married* and health factors, including infertility (16% each).

- An array of *additional factors* cited included other priorities, age, that having children was not important to them, the belief they would not be good parents, world conditions, lack of money, and career issues.

Table 4.5. Reasons for Not Having Children

Health factors	16%
Not being married	16
Other priorities	9
Age	8
Not important	8
Would be poor parents	7
Condition of the world	7
Finances	6
Career issues	4
No one main reason	8
Other	11
Total	100

Reasons Cited for Not Having Children
Some Response Examples

...partner did not want any...no future for them...did not find suitable mate...I could not have any...not married...too old...didn't want them...poor health...I'm too selfish...low priority...we wanted our freedom from that responsibility...not important to me...I would be too strict on them...it just didn't work out...world is too shitty...no time for children...didn't marry until I was 59...it was illegal at the time...haven't had the right partner to have children with...I wouldn't be a good parent...money...too many other things I want to do in life...parents mess up kids, mine did, why continue that?...the more I'm around them, the more I dislike them...the world is not a very nice place...can't afford to pay my own bills, not ready for that kind of commitment...I'm afraid I'll hurt them emotionally...I have too many other priorities...I'm scared of the pain, the commitment, everything...too much work...I would be a bad mother...not a priority...work situation would make it difficult...not ready...planet of crazies...sexual orientation...lack of time to invest...overpopulation...I didn't think we'd be good parents...

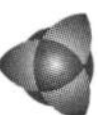

The majority of Canadians (63%) do not believe there is a particular ideal age for people who want to have children to have them.

- Among the 37% who do think there is an ideal age, the average age men view as ideal is just over 28, compared to just over 27 for women.[23]

- Adults under the age of 35 see the ideal age for starting to have children as older— about 31 for males and 30 for females. Older adults see those ideal ages as three or four years younger – a bit over 27 for men and around 26 for women.

- Most respondents who offer an ideal age for having children are reflecting the age at which they themselves started "having kids." The average age was 27.7 for men, and 25.7 for women (26.7 overall); the median ages were 27 and 25 respectively.

Canadians are far less inhibited when it comes to what factors they think should be important when people choose to have children. We gave participants a list of nine possible factors, along with the opportunity to add another key factor that may have been omitted.

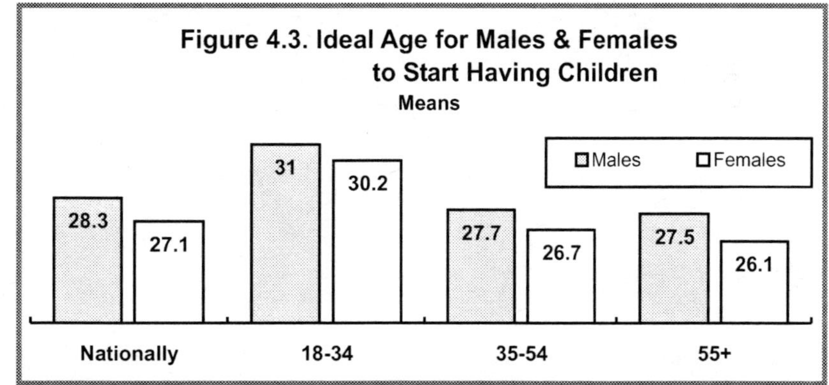

- People are nearly unanimous in pointing to three essential factors that should be involved in the decision to have children: having *enough time* for them, *recognizing the responsibilities* associated with being a parent, and the *strength of one's relationship*.

- Three additional factors are seen as important to more than 8 in 10 people: being *able to afford them, family planning*, and seeing children as providing a *sense of fulfillment.*

- The desire for *companionship* is viewed as important by about 6 in 10 respondents.

- Less important motivating factors in the minds of most include carrying on the *family name* and having children as a means of *expanding social ties*.

- Variations in citing the top six of the nine factors are minor. However, the *desire for companionship* is somewhat more frequently mentioned by people outside Quebec, by men, and by people 55 and over. The importance of *carrying on the family name* is noted more often by men than women, and by people over 55 than younger adults. Quebec respondents are quite a bit more likely than people elsewhere to see the expansion of *social ties* as being an important determinant in having children.

Table 4.6. Important Considerations in People Having Children

% Indicating "Very Important" or "Somewhat Important"

	Nationally	ROC	Quebec	Women	Men	18-34	35-54	55+
Having enough time for them	97%	97	98	98	97	98	97	96
Recognition of responsibilities involved in being a parent	96	95	99	97	95	95	96	97
Strength of one's relationship	95	95	95	95	95	95	96	94
Being able to afford them	87	86	88	89	84	92	83	86
Careful family planning	86	88	81	86	87	90	86	84
A sense of fulfillment	83	82	85	82	84	79	83	86
Desire for companionship	58	61	48	52	64	54	56	65
Carrying on the family name	39	38	46	31	48	35	35	51
A desire to expand social ties	34	29	50	30	37	33	34	35

Considerations in Having Children: Some "Other" Thoughts

...good health...a love for children ...devotion...sharing your love produces your children...strong moral beliefs...ability to put children first...not overpopulating the world...willingness to accept all the responsibilities...commitment for life...mental stability...understanding the importance of children in the cycle of life...unselfishness...I wish couples would really examine why they want children...having unconditional love...the willingness to give of yourself selflessly for the next 18+ years...

What People Want for Their Children

As part of our effort to better understand parents, we asked, *"What is your greatest hope for your kids?"* The question was open-ended. We found that almost all the respondents mentioned at least two "greatest hopes" for their offspring.

Almost 1 in 2 said "happiness," while 1 in 5 said "health." What's interesting is the extent to which more specific traits were also mentioned.

- About 13% say their "greatest hope" is that their children will be *successful*, and speak in terms of achievement, prosperity and money.

- Close to the same number see *fulfillment* as extremely important expressed as things like realizing their dreams and living up to their potential.

- About 10% emphasize *good character*, mentioning things like values, morals and virtues.

- Just under 10% say that "their greatest hope" lies with good relationships love, marriage, companionship, and so on. About the same number want their children to experience a good quality of life lives that are full and balanced.

- Around 5% mention an array of "greatest hopes" relating to security (world peace, personal safety), *good citizenship* (community involvement, contributing to life), *religion* and a *good family life* (having children, being good parents).

- Smaller numbers emphasize education and leading productive lives.

Table 4.7. Greatest Hopes for One's "Kids"

Happiness	47%
Health	18
Success	13
Fulfillment	12
Good character	10
Good relationships	8
Good quality of life	8
Physical security	6
Good citizens	4
Religious commitment	4
Good family life	4
Good careers	3
Education	3
Productive lives	2

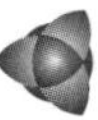

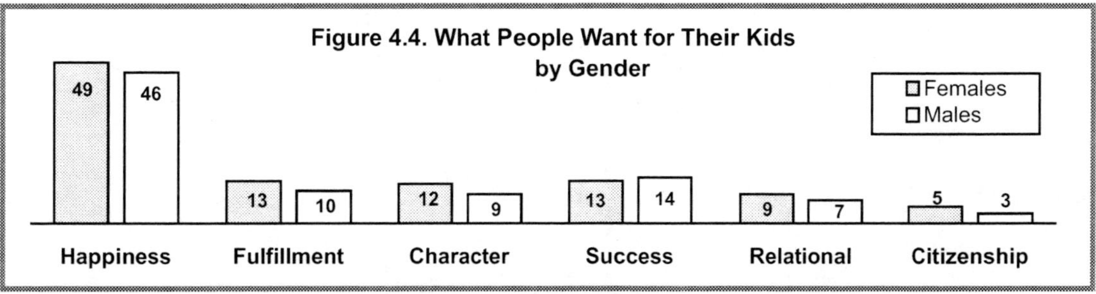

Canadians' Greatest Hopes for Their Kids
Some Response Examples

...healthy, happy, productive lives...stable life, love and reach their goals...a good education so she can have a good job that she likes...happiness...love and confidence...happy and capable of getting through life...to grow as people and be healthy...to be honest and forgiving...health, happiness and a happy home for their children... financial security...to be successful in life...that they be able to fend for themselves...a long healthy happy life...that they realize their dreams...good education, good career and good family life...health and happiness...education and good jobs...love, health, prosperity...enjoy life and be somewhat successful financially...that they be happy, safe, secure...love, compassion for others, be global in their thinking...that they will grow up feeling loved and confident...that they be successful and happy...financial security and good family values...pride, honour, success...happy, stable home life and financial stability...a rewarding life, whatever they do...good quality of life...that they be decent people...that they are fulfilled in all aspects of their lives...

In light of such expressed hopes for their children, it is worthwhile to briefly look at some of the goal-like values of parents and other Canadians—what they themselves say they want out of life.

- Two core values stand out—the importance people give to *relationships—family life*, being loved and friends—and, almost paradoxically, the importance they give to *freedom*, which for many includes privacy.

- Next in importance to relationships and freedom are more material goals *a comfortable life and success.*

- Of less importance: appreciation for *spirituality*, a *rewarding career*, personal *religious faith and involvement in one's community*.

- *Variations* are relatively few. More *women* than men place importance on being loved and privacy; more *younger adults* than older adults say friends and career are significant for them, while fewer say the same about family life generally; and *people with children* are more inclined than others to value family life highly, and less likely to see friends and careers as extremely important.

Table 4.8. Adult Values: Goals

"How important are the following to you?"

% Indicating "Very Important"

	Nationally	Females	Males	18-34	35-54	55+	Have Children	No Children
Freedom*	89%	90	88	88	90	90	88	90
Family life generally	86	90	82	79	87	92	92	71
Being loved	85	90	79	85	85	83	85	83
A comfortable life*	62	61	65	66	62	61	60	65
Friends	61	65	56	70	55	60	54	70
Privacy	59	65	53	58	59	60	59	59
Success in what you do	49	48	49	52	44	53	48	51
Appreciation for spirituality	42	46	37	40	37	50	43	37
A rewarding career	39	36	42	46	34	39	35	45
Your personal religious faith	33	38	29	27	28	48	35	28
Involvement in your community	20	21	19	17	19	25	20	19

*Data source: Project Canada 2000.

These values help to clarify how Canadians see how the happiness and well-being they want for their children is achieved. The key, for many, lies with good social ties, freedom and the material comfort associated with success.

Despite only 20% of adults saying that involvement in the community is "very important" to them, over one-half indicate they are currently involved in various community activities, including volunteer work.

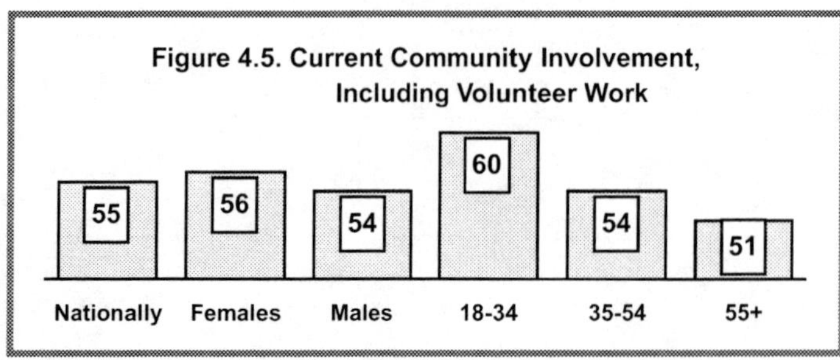

What Kinds of People Parents Hope Their Children Will Become

Basic to any civil society is the ability of people to be able to get along with each other. **We asked our respondents about the importance they place on instilling in children a number of basic interpersonal goals and some basic ways of reaching those objectives.**

- Canadians are nearly unanimous in endorsing the importance of children learning to be *responsible* for their actions.

- Some 8 in 10 feel the same way about traits such as *getting* along with other people, *compassion* and *good manners*.

- About 7 in 10 think that it is important to instill ideas such as being a *good citizen*, respecting the *environment* and *individuality.*

- Similar levels of agreement exist for teaching children about the importance of *accepting diversity*, *respecting authority* and leaving the *world in better shape*.

- *Women* are more inclined than men to endorse a number of traits: concern for others, respect for the environment, individuality and acceptance of diversity. *Older adults* are more likely than younger adults to think citizenship and respect for authority should be instilled in children, and less likely to emphasize the importance of children accepting diversity.

Table 4.9. Most Important Children's Values: Interpersonal Goals

"How important do you think it is for parents to instill these values in their children?"

% Indicating "Very Important"

	Nationally	Females	Males	18-34	35-54	55+	Have Children	No Children
Responsibility for one's actions	92%	95	89	93	91	91	92	92
Getting along with others	84	87	80	79	84	88	86	77
Concern for others	80	87	73	83	78	80	79	83
Good manners	79	80	77	74	81	80	82	71
Being a good citizen	75	79	70	66	75	84	79	66
Respect for the environment	73	78	67	74	71	75	72	73
Individuality	72	78	67	74	74	69	72	73
Acceptance of diversity	69	76	61	82	65	61	64	79
Respect for authority	68	71	65	60	69	74	73	58
Leaving world in better shape	67	71	62	67	67	68	67	67

- *People with children* tend to give more emphasis than people without children to values such as good manners, being good citizens and respecting authority fewer place high importance on *instilling acceptance of diversity*.

And what values, in turn, do Canadians see as leading to such good interpersonal life—the means to such goals? Here, there is less consensus.

- Almost everyone endorses the importance of *instilling honesty*.

- Around 85% say the same about *politeness*, *reliability* and *forgiveness*.

- Some 75% think traits like *morality*, *generosity*, *working hard* and *friendliness* are important to instill.

- The figures drop to about 65% for *humour*, *sensitivity* and the need to *follow rules*.

Generally speaking, *women* are more likely than men to place importance on instilling all of these characteristics. The same tends to be true for *parents* versus people without children. Significant *age* differences are limited to older adults placing more importance on children coming to value reliability, morality, and the need to follow rules. It may be noteworthy than only one in two Gen-Xers and people without children think that it's "very important" to instill the need to follow rules.

Table 4.10. Most Important Children's Values: Interpersonal Means

"How important do you think it is for parents to instill these values in their children?"

% Indicating "Very Important"

	Nationally	Females	Males	18-34	35-54	55+	Have Children	No Children
Honesty	98%	98	97	98	98	98	98	98
Politeness	85	87	83	81	86	87	87	81
Reliability	84	86	82	77	86	89	88	76
Forgiveness	83	84	81	81	85	81	84	81
Morality	78	81	75	75	75	85	80	74
Generosity	77	82	72	79	79	73	78	76
Working hard	76	78	74	76	75	76	77	73
Friendliness	73	78	68	79	71	71	72	74
Humour	68	74	61	64	72	65	68	64
Sensitivity	67	72	63	62	71	66	69	64
Need to follow rules	64	66	62	52	67	71	70	49

Some variations by age in the importance of these "civility goals and means" seem to point to intergenerational changes in values.

- However, 89% of Canadians say, *"my values are fairly similar to those of my parents."*

- What's more, no less than 94% of Canadian parents think that *"my children hold values fairly similar to me,"* with little variation in the claim between Pre-Boomer (95%), Boomer (94%), and Gen-Xer (90%) parents. Differences between males and females are negligible for both items.

Figure 4.6. My Values Are Fairly Similar to My Parents' by Age

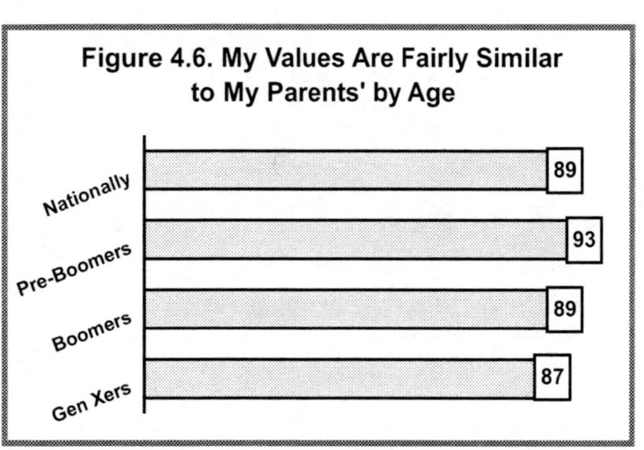

A closing footnote on value sources: we asked Canadians the open-ended question, ***"Where do you think young people get their values today?"*** Two responses dominated: (1) the media and (2) the family. To a lesser extent, they pointed to young peoples' friends, the school and a number of other "minor" sources.

When they were asked, ***"Where do you think young people should get their values today?"*** they overwhelmingly pointed to the family, followed by school, religious groups, and friends. Most people maintain that neither the media nor the Internet should be a significant source of values for youth.

An interesting argument – but frankly, seemingly an impossible dream. We will return to this important issue later.

Table 4.11. The Top Seven Perceived Sources of Young Peoples' Values

Source	%
1. TV and other media	39%
2. Family	38
3. Friends	27
4. School	12
5. Internet	3
6. Neighbourhood	2
7. Religion	1

Table 4.12. What the Top Seven Sources of Youth Values *Should* Be

Source	%
1. Family	86%
2. School	14
3. Religion	14
4. Friends	9
5. TV and other media	2
6. Neighbourhood	2
7. Internet	<1

When we asked **Canadian teenagers** between the ages of 15 and 19 for their perception of what factors in general influence their lives, they provided a "top ten" list of their own.

—And finally, in our current adult survey, we asked **our respondents** what they view as **their own values**. The results below speak for themselves.

Table 4.13. The Top Ten Outside Sources of Influence, According to Teenagers

Source	%
1. Family	63%
2. Friends	39
3. Music	25
4. God/supernatural force	23
5. Another adult you respect	20
6. What you read	14
7. Television	11
8. School	8
9. People in power	7
10. Internet	5

Source: Bibby, Project Teen Canada 2000.

Table 4.14. The Top Seven Sources of Adult Values

Source	%
1. My personal beliefs	25%
2. Family	19
3. Religion & God	19
4. Consequences for others	16
5. My personal judgment	11
6. Impact on me	3
7. Other people	2
*Media	<1

THE LONGER LOOK

The Enjoyment of Children by Select Variables: 1985 & 2000

% Indicating they are receiving "a great deal" of enjoyment from their children

	2000	1985
NATIONALLY*	**72%**	**82**
18-34	77	85
55+	73	84
35-54	69	78
Females	77	83
Males	68	80
Degree-Plus	77	76
High School	72	79
<High School	70	84
White	72	82
Other Races	69	86
Born in Canada	74	***
Born Outside Canada	68	***
Satisfied with financial situation**	73	82
Not satisfied with financial situation	69	83
Lack of time a cause for concern	75	83
Lack of time not a cause for concern	70	80

*National enjoyment levels were 76% in 1990 and 73% in 1995.
**"Pretty well" or "More or less" satisfied, vs. "Not very" or "Not satisfied at all."

Source: Reginald W. Bibby, Project Canada Survey Series.

Summary Note

Some 70% of Canadian adults today have an average of approximately 2.5 children. Both figures are down slightly from the 1970s, primarily the result, it seems, of people in the 18-to 34-year-old cohort waiting longer to have fewer children. Having or not having children follows predictable marital status and age patterns. The presence of children—versus the number—is as common in Quebec as elsewhere, and much more common among previously married cohabitants than couples who have never been married.

Parents say that finances and health were or are among the major determinants of the number of children they have or plan to have. Age and what they could or can handle emotionally also stand out as important factors for many. Only about 20% see the matter as being resolved by chance. That said, just two in three parents report that all their children were actually planned—leaving more than a little room for chance. After two children, lack of planning increases with the number of children one has had. Young adults say they expect their planning to have better results.

Some nine in ten people acknowledge that having children is something that was or is important for them to do in their lifetimes. Those who do not intend to have children most often cite not being married and health factors as the main reasons for their decisions. However, about 20% also indicate that their choices are because they don't see having children as important or because they have other priorities.

The majority of Canadians do not believe there is an ideal age for people to have children, seemingly regarding such a decision as an individual one. However, they are not lost for opinions on key factors that should characterize people who want to be parents, notably having sufficient time, recognizing the responsibilities involved, and having a strong relationship with one's partner. They also see adequate finances and family planning as particularly important.

Parents typically want their children to be happy and healthy. More specifically, reflecting their own values, most want their children to experience fulfilling lives characterized by good relationships and physical comfort that in turn reflects success. Less important but still important to many are things like a good education and a rewarding career, spirituality and religious faith, and involvement in one's community.

Canadians—led by parents—recognize the need to instill values that make up a good interpersonal life. They include "goal-like values such as responsibility, getting along with people, compassion, good manners, and being a good citizen. In addition, "means-like values" like honesty, politeness, morality, working hard, and friendliness are also seen as important. Consensus is lower on the need to instill traits such as sensitivity, respect for authority and, in particular, the need to follow rules.

Despite their concern about value sources, Canadians tend to think that their values are much like their parents, and that their children's values, in turn, are much like their own. Here, in the midst of considerable cultural change, most believe that, within their families, at least, the values "that really matter" are persisting across generations.

Reflections:
How Canadians Feel About Children

It would be difficult to overestimate the importance that Canadians place on children. Most people see them as indispensable to family life. No less than 97% acknowledge that it is important for them to have children in their lifetimes. When they do not have children, it is, as often as not, because they have little choice in the matter. In all, 99% report that their children are sources of considerable enjoyment—albeit, at times, also sources of a fair amount strain.

Given the importance they place on children, Canadians feel that people need to take parenthood very seriously. We have been told that individuals need to make sure that they must have enough time for children and recognize the responsibilities involved in being a parent. In addition, would-be parents need to have strong relationships, be able to look after their children financially and plan their arrival. In their own cases, the number of children that people have had or plan to have has been/is based first and foremost on the strength of their relationships, finances and their health. The majority do not see any specific ideal age for becoming parents; what is more important is that people exhibit appropriate parental traits.

More than anything else, Canadians want their children to be happy. They vary, of course, on how they think such happiness is achieved. But overall they want them to experience physical, emotional and material well-being, with many emphasizing their spiritual well-being as well.

Canadians also want their children to be responsible. They give considerable emphasis to the social well-being of their children. They want them to be able to relate well to others—family, friends, and people more generally. Eight in ten parents think that it's very important to instill in their children the need to be good citizens.

The consternation about changing values may be largely unwarranted. In 2000, about 55% of people across the country maintained that "values have been changing for the worse." Yet, our current survey shows that most Canadians think that their own values are fairly similar to those of their parents, and that their children's values are fairly similar to their own. What's more, even though adults think that media rival the family as the source of values for young people, teenagers say the controversy is a non-issue: their primary source of influence—by a wide margin—is, they say, the family.

Fifty years ago, an old pop song familiar to many readers proclaimed: "Love and marriage...go together like a horse and carriage," adding, "This I tell you brother, you can't have one without the other." Our findings so far suggest that the old lyric needs to be modified. Love may not always go along with marriage anymore. But love and parenthood do. **Almost everyone wants to have children—still**.

Some Issues Raised by the Findings

1. The tremendous importance Canadians place on children suggests that issues that affect children warrant extremely high societal priority and that related initiatives will receive extremely high societal support.

2. Having children is seen as a great responsibility. What as a society can be done to ensure that parenthood "is not entered into lightly"?

3. What kinds of contributions are Canada's major public and private institutions making to support families as they try to instill in their children the importance of strong interpersonal relationships and civic duty?

Parenting and Parents

There appears to be considerable difficulty moving from the ideal to the real when it comes to parenting. We saw earlier, for example, that 99% of Canadians agree that parents need to take equal responsibility for raising their children. However, we also saw that raising children is one of the top areas of tension for couples. Similar disparities between the ideal and real are apparent in such areas as child care and the care of aging parents.

The survey asked some direct questions in a number of these areas to try to better understand the current nature of the gulf between the real and ideal in parenting.

When I Was a Child...

As we noted at the beginning of the report, Canadians have known diverse family experiences as children themselves. Still, the vast majority of respondents—84%—indicate that they were raised by their biological mothers and fathers.

- Another 9% were raised by their mother, and a further 2% by their mother and a stepfather.

- The remaining 7% knew a variety of home experiences when they were growing up, including adoption, being raised by their fathers alone and sometimes with a stepmother present. In other instances, their homes included their biological mother or father and an unmarried partner. In still other instances, they were raised by grandparents, aunts and uncles, foster parents or other individuals.

Table 5.1. Home Situation As Children

"Who primarily raised you?"

	Nationally	18-34	35-54	55+
Mother and father	84%	77	88	87
Mother only	9	16	6	7
Mother and stepfather	2	3	2	1
Adoptive parents	1	1	1	1
Father only	1	1	<1	1
Father and stepmother	<1	<1	<1	1
Mother and her male partner	<1	1	0	0
Father and his female partner	<1	<1	0	0
Other	2	1	2	2
Totals	100	100	100	100

Most Canadian adults remember their home lives in fairly positive terms.

- No less than 95% maintain that, *"All in all, I think my parents did a good job of raising me."* Variations are insignificant by gender and age of respondents.

- Such a positive appraisal varies somewhat with home situation: it is highest among people raised by both their mothers and their fathers. Nevertheless, it is also high in other situations as well.

Figure 5.1. "My Parents Did A Good Job of Raising Me"

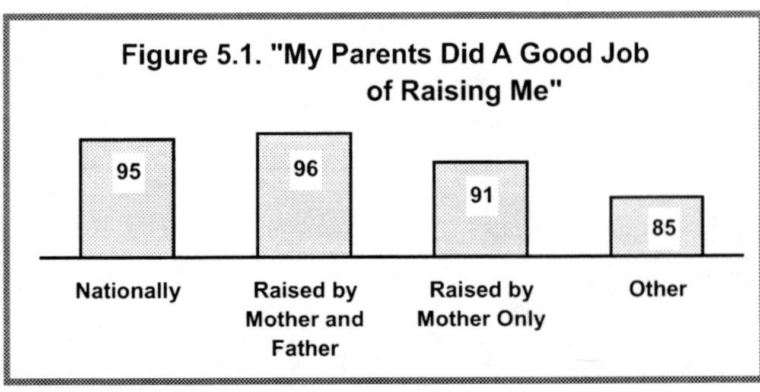

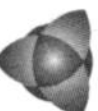

As we noted at the beginning of the report, Canadians have known diverse family experiences as children themselves. Still, the vast majority of respondents—84%—indicate that they were raised by their biological mothers and fathers.

- Another 9% were raised by their mother, and a further 2% by their mother and a stepfather.

- The remaining 7% knew a variety of home experiences when they were growing up, including adoption, being raised by their fathers alone and sometimes with a stepmother present. In other instances, their homes included their biological mother or father and an unmarried partner. In still other instances, they were raised by grandparents, aunts and uncles, foster parents or other individuals.

Most Canadian adults remember their home lives in fairly positive terms.

- No less than 95% maintain that, *"All in all, I think my parents did a good job of raising me."* Variations are insignificant by gender and age of respondents.

- Such a positive appraisal varies somewhat with home situation: it is highest among people raised by both their mothers and their fathers. Nevertheless, it is also high in other situations as well.

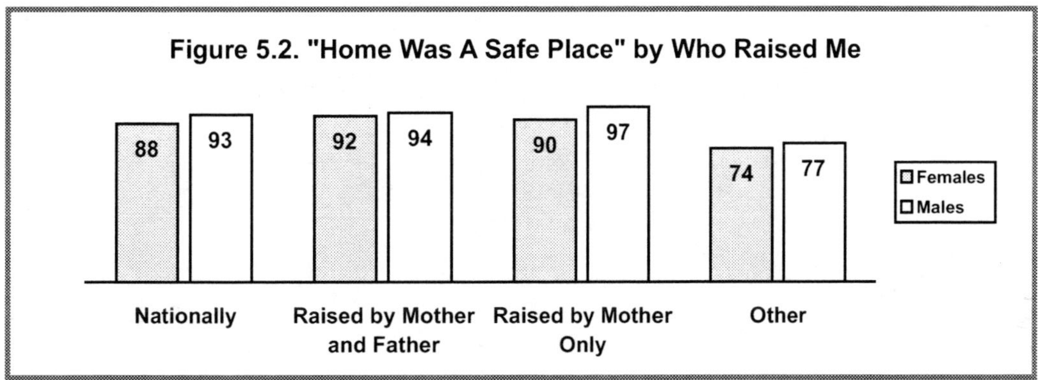

Some other "fast facts" on the families of origin of today's adults follow.

- Adults say they had an average of 2.7 *brothers and sisters*—with the average just under two for those under the age of 35.

- When they turned 16, in 93% of cases both of their biological *parents were still alive*. But 5% had lost their fathers, 2% their mothers and just under 1% both parents.

- Ninety per cent say that when they were growing up, "home was always a safe place." The downside of such a positive finding is that home nevertheless was not a safe place for one in ten adults—12% of women and 7% of men. Recollections of home as a safe sanctuary differ little whether or not people were raised by their mother and father, or their mother only. There is, however, a noteworthy drop in such a view for those who were raised in other settings. In all three upbringing configurations, women are slightly less likely than men to report that home was a safe place.

- About 73% of Canadians say that they were *spanked as children*, with the level higher for males (77%) than females (69%). However, spanking is not associated with safety at home: to the extent that it occurred, it took place equally in "safe" and "unsafe" home settings. Somewhat surprisingly, Gen-Xers are just as likely as Boomers and Pre-Boomers to report that they were spanked. This may reflect objective reality as well as heightened sensitivity to the subject.

As they reflect on how much enjoyment versus how much strain they experience or experienced with their mothers, fathers and siblings, about 7 in 10 Canadians say those individuals, on balance, brought them a high level of enjoyment and very little strain.

- Another 2 in 10 indicate that each of the three contributed enjoyment, but also were the sources of quite a bit of strain.

- The remaining 1 in 10 say that parents and siblings did not bring much enjoyment, and contributed varying amounts of strain.

People who have been raised by *both* their mothers and fathers are more likely than others to report high levels of enjoyment and less strain in their relationships with both parents, as well as in their ties with their brothers and sisters.

- A solid majority of 8 in 10 who were raised by their mothers express positive sentiments about their relationships with their mothers—but 4 in 10 also say they experienced high levels of strain. Some 56% of those raised by their mothers say they experienced enjoyment from their fathers, while 50% acknowledge strain.

- People who grew up in *other parent and guardian settings*—where applicable—tend to report lower enjoyment levels and higher strain levels for both mothers and fathers than people who were raised by both parents. The enjoyment-strain balance for brothers and sisters, while not as positive as in two-parent settings, still is more positive in such circumstances than it is for mothers or fathers. Here, positive bonds between children living in similar settings seem to be frequently more prevalent and enduring than such ties with either parent.

Table 5.2. Enjoyment and Strain Associated With Parents and Siblings by Family Background

"On balance, how much ENJOYMENT and how much STRAIN would you say you experience/or experienced with…"

	Lots/Quite a Bit Enjoyment, Very Little Strain	Quite a Bit Enjoyment, Quite Bit Strain	Not Very Much Enjoyment, Very Little Strain	Not Very Much Enjoyment, Quite Bit Strain	TOTALS
NATIONALLY					
Your mother	70%	20	4	6	100
Your father	67	17	6	10	100
Your brother(s)/sister(s)	69	18	8	5	100
Your Mother					
Raised by Both	73	18	4	5	100
Raised by Mothers	59	33	2	6	100
Raised: Other	50	25	12	13	100
Your Father					
Raised by Both	72	16	5	7	100
Raised by Mothers	38	16	12	34	100
Raised: Other	48	21	9	22	100
Your Siblings					
Raised by Both	71	18	7	4	100
Raised by Mothers	64	21	10	5	100
Raised: Other	62	21	12	5	100

Raising Children

No less than 99% of Canadian parents feel that, overall, they did or are doing a good job of raising their children—slightly higher than what 95% said about how their parents raised them.

The fact that an increasingly large number of couples with children are both employed outside the home obviously has raised important questions about child rearing and child care.[24]

More than 8 in 10 employed parents with children under the age of 20 say that they think they *have found a fairly good balance between their jobs and their children.*

- At the same time, about 40% of employed parents—led by married fathers and cohabitating or divorced/separated mothers—acknowledge that *their children probably don't think they spend enough time with them.* Just 31% of employed married mothers and 28% of mothers who are not employed express the same feelings.

***

- For all the assumptions about the importance of careers, the survey found that 80% of employed parents with children claim, *"I'd stay home and raise my children if I could afford to."* That includes 85% of men with children. Obviously "staying home" doesn't preclude people working for pay from home. But at minimum, it does say a great deal about where parents would like to be physically located.

- Further, 70% of these "mothers at home" say they *would work part-time* if they could afford to; employment opportunities and child care issues may be among the key reasons they don't.[25] Among parents who are employed full-time, the part-time preference is strong—expressed by 90% of married mothers and 84% of married fathers, as well as all the mothers in our sample who are cohabiting, divorced or separated.

Table 5.3. Some Parental Thoughts About Raising Children and Being Employed

% Strongly Agreeing or Agreeing

	NOT EMPLOYED	*EMPLOYED PARENTS*				
	Mothers	ALL	Mothers Married	Fathers Married	Mothers Cohab	Mothers Div-Sep
Overall, I think I did/am doing a good job of raising my children	99%	99	100	99	100	100
I've found a pretty good balance between my job & my children	***	83	82	83	93	80
My children probably think I don't spend enough time with them	28	41	31	44	47	44
I'd stay home and raise my children if I could afford to		80	82	85	81	54
I'd work part time and raise my children if I could afford to	70	90	90	84	100	100

There are pronounced differences between parents who are employed and those who are not regarding time, household work and help raising children.

- Those who work outside the home are considerably more likely to say they never seem to have *enough time*, and are not spending enough time with their children. What's more, concerns about inadequate time are expressed by more married women than married men.[26]

- Employed women—married and otherwise—differ from men in expressing concern about having to do most of the *household work* themselves. This concern is also voiced by a higher proportion of "mothers at home" than mothers employed outside the home. Staying home, it seems, often has the effect of women feeling or being made to feel that the gender division of labour calls for household duties to be largely—even entirely—theirs.

- About 16% of employed mothers say they are troubled that they are *not receiving much help* raising their children; 9% of employed fathers express the same concern.

- *Divorced mothers* who are employed outside the home are considerably more likely than other parents to say that they are troubled by not having much help either with their children or their household work.

Concerns about balancing employment and the well-being of children raises the age-old question of whether or not—in two-parent situations—one should stay home and take primary responsibility for raising children.

- Nine in 10 Canadians feel one parent should stay home in the case of *preschoolers*, with little difference by either age or gender.

- The figures drop to just over 6 in 10 when children are in *elementary school*, and to 3 in 10 when they are *older.* Support for one parent staying home in these latter two instances is lowest among adults under 35, and increases with age. Male-female differences are minor.

Table 5.4. Some Parental Concerns About Time and Division of Labour

% Concerned "A Great Deal" or "Quite A Bit"

	NOT EMPLOYED	EMPLOYED PARENTS				
	Mothers	ALL	Mothers Married	Fathers Married	Mothers Cohab	Mothers Div-Sep
Never seeming to have enough time	49%	67	77	58	65	58
Not spending enough time with my children	19	46	55	40	61	40
Having to spend so much time on my job	***	36	44	28	54	22
Having to do most of the household work myself	39	23	33	10	25	54
Not getting much help in raising my children	10	16	16	9	14	35

We asked those respondents who indicated that one person should stay home the tough question: *"Who do you think that [person] should be?"*

- Virtually everyone maintains the person staying home should be *either* the *mother* or father, or the mother; less than 1% see *dads* as the best choice.

- The mother is particularly preferred by *adults over 55*. She is also the number one choice of 1 in 4 adults 35 to 54 and 1 in 7 of those under 35—as well as 35% of *men* compared to 26% of *women*.

What's the rationale behind these choices? In the case of those who say "either," many reiterate the idea that it is good to have one person at home but don't place importance on that person being either the mother or father.

- Some say it is an issue of equality, while others say both are equally capable of doing the job.

- Others point to the key criteria including things like career and other circumstances, while still others say it should depend on who can carry out the stay-at-home role better as well as who is happier playing it.

Table 5.5. One Parent Should Stay Home

"Ideally, do you think it is preferable for one parent to stay home and take primary responsibility for raising children when they are…"

	NAT	18-34	35-54	55+	Women	Men
Pre-schoolers						
Yes, definitely	70%	66	67	79	72	69
Yes, probably	20	25	21	13	18	21
Not necessarily	9	8	11	7	9	9
No	1	1	1	1	1	1
In elementary						
Yes, definitely	27	17	26	40	27	27
Yes, probably	37	37	37	37	38	37
Not necessarily	30	37	31	20	29	30
No	6	9	6	3	6	6
Beyond elementary						
Yes, definitely	9	5	8	15	11	8
Yes, probably	20	15	20	25	20	20
Not necessarily	51	51	54	47	50	52
No	20	29	18	13	19	20

Table 5.6. One Parent Should Stay Home by Gender and Age

"Who do you think that it should be?"

	NAT	18-34	35-54	55+	Women	Men
Either	69	85	73	48	73	65
The mother	30	15	27	51	26	35
The father	<1	0	0	<1	<1	0
It depends	<1	<1	<1	<1	<1	<1

Those who feel the mother should stay home tend to take the position that she is better suited for the task—in large part because that's "the way things should be." Some also note that such a resolution will have less of a negative financial impact on the home, obviously assuming that the father is earning more money—a situation that many people over 55 experienced most of their lives.

Despite the widespread belief that one person should stay home and look after children, especially when they are preschool age, the reality is that child care is required. Often, of course, it's because both parents are either employed or going to university or college. Sometimes it's because they are single parents. In any case, what's involved are what some observers have referred to as "necessary compromises."

To the extent that parents require child care, what are their preferences? And to what extent do we see that, again, they have to make "necessary compromises"?

Table 5.7. Reasons for the Stay-At-Home Choice

Either	**58%**
Good to have one	16
Equality	11
Both capable	10
Career	8
Circumstances	6
Who is better	5
Who is happier	2
Mother	**25**
Best suited	9
Finances	5
It's her role	4
Natural	4
Best Bond	3
Other	**17**
Total	**100**

Canadians Who Think One Parent Should Stay Home
Some Response Examples

Either

...either, because no one can take a parent's place...love and support is needed 24 hours a days...family is a partnership and partners are equally responsible...whatever works best for the family...one many be better or have better skills and patience with children...they need to work it out...depends on who wants to work...both are responsible for the well-being of the child...who makes the most money should work...the child needs to feel a belonging to each parent...should be shared equally...what each prefer...circumstances should determine...the important thing is to have someone home and available at any time...each couple must decide what is best...someone else is raising them if you're not...

The Mother

...because she is more patient and tolerant...she is a better nurturer, especially during illness...the man should be the bread-winner...she is more qualified...a female is more caring than a male...the place of the mother is in the home...women have natural maternal instincts...because it's time we got back to basics...key maternal relationship continues from birth...she has more patience...though there are exceptions men tend to earn more income...bonding...she usually provides the most stability ...the mother is a natural care-giver...small children seem closer to their mother...she usually understands the care of a child better...she does it best...

We put the question to Canadians as a whole: ***"If you and your partner were/are employed outside the home and you had these choices for the care of your preschool children, which would be your top 5 choices?"*** We posed seven child care possibilities and asked them to rank them "1 to 5." We then calculated the average scores for each of the seven options.

We found that, **in an ideal world, the number one choice is one's partner, followed by one's parent, then another relative. Rounding out the top five? Home-based child care followed by a child care centre.** Failing to make the top five list were *friends* and *sitters*.

- These rankings are highly consistent by both gender and age.

- Exceptions are minor—younger adults rank child care centres ahead of home child care; adults 55 and over rank sitters ahead of friends.

Such findings suggest that the advocating of child care settings as the primary solution to the need for child care—as often seems to be the case—do not, in fact, represent the wishes of most Canadian parents. Solutions relating to partners, parents and relatives appear to be preferable to daycares.

A quick note on discipline. There has been considerable controversy in Canada in recent years about the appropriateness of spanking. We've seen that 3 in 4 adults—led by men—say they were spanked as children. How do they feel about the issue?

- Some 65% say spanking should be *legal*, while 60% say it should be *discouraged*.

- *Men* are far more likely than *women* to favour spanking being legal, and also less likely to feel spanking should be discouraged.

- Perhaps surprising to many, there is little attitudinal variation by *age*.

Table 5.8. child care Choices

"If you and your partner were/are employed outside the home and you had these choices for the care of your preschool children, which would be your TOP 5 choices?"

Rank Order of Average Scores

	Nationally	Females	Males	18-34	35-54	55+
Partner	1	1	1	1	1	1
Parent(s)	2	2	2	2	2	2
Another relative	3	3	3	3	3	3
A home daycare	4	4	4	5	4	4
A daycare centre	5	5	5	4	5	5
Friends	6	6	6	6	6	7
A sitter	7	7	7	7	7	6

Figure 5.3. Attitudes Toward Spanking by Gender

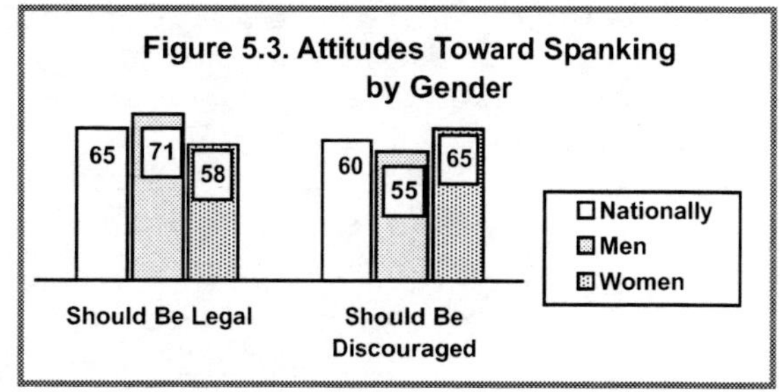

Some Additional Attitudes About Parenting

The survey attempted to confront Canadians directly on a number of other controversial topics relating to parenting.

Single Parenting

More than 7 in 10 people maintain that, generally speaking, single parents do a good job of *raising children*. Women (78%) are more likely than men (67%) to agree with that assessment, as are Gen-Xers (81%) versus Boomers and Pre-Boomers (about 68%). Partly reflecting age, some 64% of weekly religious service attendees agree, as do 75% of those who attend services less often or not at all.

Gay Parenting.

About 6 in 10 Canadians say that same sex couples can do a good job of *raising children*. There are differences between women (69%) and men (52%), and particularly pronounced differences among Gen-X adults (76%), Boomers (61%) and Pre-Boomers (42%). However, there is less support for gay couples being able to *legally adopt* children. Five in 10 Canadians agree with the idea.[27] Once again, significant differences exist between females (58%) and males (40%), and between younger adults (69%), middle-aged adults (49%) and older adults (27%). On both issues, opposition is considerably higher among weekly religious service attendees than others.[28]

New Technologies And Parenting

Scientific and technological advances in recent years have made it possible for many women to overcome difficulties and become pregnant. Other more radical developments have made human cloning a possibility. The survey probed attitudes regarding both topics.

Eighty per cent of Canadians say they approve of *new technologies* that enable women to get pregnant. While differences are small, females, adults under the age of 55, and weekly religious service attendees are more inclined to indicate their approval than others.

On the subject of cloning, a mere 6% of people across the nation feel that it should be permissible to produce children who are *human clones*. Support is marginally higher among males, younger adults and people not actively involved in religious groups than other people.[29]

Table 5.9. Attitudes on Select Parenting Topics by Gender, Age and Religious Service Attendan ce

% Strongly Agreeing or Agreeing

	NAT	Females	Males	18-34	35-54	55+	Wkly	<Wkly
On balance, single parents do a good job of raising children	72%	78	67	81	69	67	64	75
Same sex couples can do a good job of raising children	61	69	52	76	61	42	37	69
Gay couples should be able to legally adopt children	48	58	40	69	49	27	22	58
I approve new technologies that enable women to get pregnant	80	82	77	82	82	74	70	83
It should be permissible produce children who are human clones	6	3	9	8	5	3	2	7

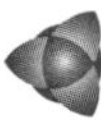

Apart from individual social characteristics, regional variations are worth noting.

- *British Columbia* residents are the most likely to feel single parents do a good job of raising children, and that same-sex couples can raise children well and should be able to adopt. They also are slightly more likely than people elsewhere to approve of new technologies that enhance the possibility of pregnancy.

- *Quebec* respondents—who throughout the survey have tended to offer more liberal attitudes on most subjects than people in the rest of the country—are somewhat *less likely* than others to agree that single parents do a good job of raising children. However, they are second only to BC in their approval of gay parenting and adoption.

- Reservations about single parenting are held by only a minority of people elsewhere, with concern highest on the *Prairies* (28%) followed by *Ontario* (25%).

- Support for gay parenting is lower on the *Prairies* (49%) than elsewhere (63%). Support for gay adoption is also lowest on the Prairies along with the *Atlantic* region (41%). On these two gay-related issues, *Ontario* residents tend to be in the middle of the regional extremes.

Table 5.10. Attitudes on Select Parenting Topics by Region

% Strongly Agreeing or Agreeing

	NAT	BC	PR	ON	PQ	AT
On balance, single parents do a good job of raising children	72%	79	72	75	62	81
Same sex couples can do a good job of raising children	61	74	49	60	64	57
Gay couples should be able to legally adopt children	48	64	41	47	51	41
I approve new technologies that enable women to get pregnant	80	84	80	77	80	79
It should be permissible produce children who are human clones	6	6	4	5	7	7

The higher levels of resistance on the Prairies to gay parenting and homosexuality more generally are associated with a lower proportion of gays and lesbians in the three western provinces. Cause and effect here seem indistinguishable.

Figure 5.4. Sexual Orientation by Region

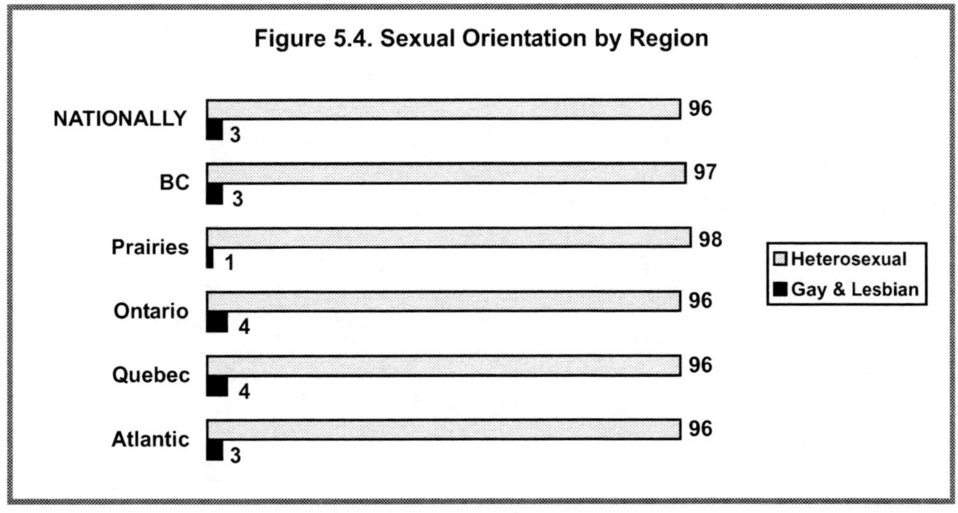

Aging Parents

A source of concern for many Canadians is the need for care of aging parents. By way of putting the magnitude of the problem into perspective, consider the following.

Facts Set 1: Living Parents

- Slightly less than 5 in 10 adults say that *both* of their parents are *alive*.

- Two in 10 report that only their *mother* is alive, and less than 1 in 10 say their *fathers* are living but not their mothers.

- *Both* parents of the remaining 3 in 10 are *deceased*.

Figure 5.5. Canadians' Parents

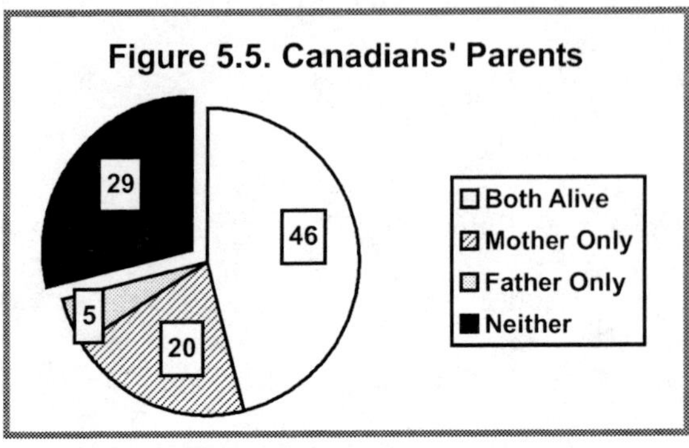

Facts Set 2: Parents in Need

- Some 75% of *adults 55 and over* have a parent or two parents who are alive, as do about 80% of *Boomer adults* who are 35-54.

- If one adds, on average, about 25 years to the children's ages, that means we are talking about *parents* who are anywhere from *about 60 to 80 or older.*

- Accordingly, more than 50% of Pre-Boomers 55 years and over who have a living mother or father indicate their parents *require "some care" or "considerable care."* About 25% of Boomers say the same thing about their mothers and around 20% say the same thing about their fathers.

- Moreover, about 20% of adults 55 and older inform us that their parents—led by their mothers—require *"a considerable amount of their time and energy,"* an admission made by over 10% of Boomers. In addition, 8% of older adults also say their parents require "a fair amount" of their money, a reality similarly noted by about 5% of 35 to 54-year-olds.

Table 5.11. Parents' Status by Age of Adult Offspring

	NAT	55+	35-54	18-34
Both Alive	46%	4	46	88
Mother only	20	18	30	10
Father only	5	3	7	2
Neither	29	75	17	<1
Mother requires:				
much care	5	15	7	1
some care	13	37	17	2
much my time & energy	9	21	11	5
fair amount my money	4	8	5	1
Father requires:				
much care	4	13	5	1
some care	9	38	13	3
much my time & energy	5	16	7	2
fair amount my money	2	8	3	<1

Facts Set 3: Where Aging Parents Live

- About 6 in 10 of the parents of Pre-Boomers still are living in their own dwellings, about 2 in 10 are in seniors' residences, and 1 in 10 are in nursing homes or chronic care hospitals. Smaller numbers live with survey respondents or other relatives.

- Close to 9 in 10 of the parents of Boomers still live in their own houses or apartments, with much fewer numbers living elsewhere at this point.[30]

Table 5.12. Where Aging Parents Are Living by Age of Adult Offspring

	55+	35-54
Own house or apartment	61%	86
Seniors' residence	23	6
Nursing home/chronic care	8	2
With you	3	3
With another relative	5	2
With a friend	<1	1
Totals	100	100

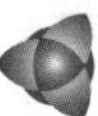

Significantly, 89% of Canadians say that they would be willing to look after their parents "if they needed me to do so." This outlook is favoured across virtually every imaginable social background and demographic variable.

They include:

- region, with minor variations
- gender
- age
- marital status
- single versus dual careers
- who one was raised by
- religious group involvement.

I emphasize the pervasiveness of this finding because I want to come back to it when we look at the kinds of priorities governments and our society thinks we should have in mind when it comes to looking after elderly parents.

Some adults are doing more than promising. As we saw in section one of the report, 4% of adults say that they have a parent or grandparent who has lived with them for more than one year—with the figures 4% for Gen-Xers, 6% for Boomers, and 2% for Pre-Boomers. When asked, 55% say the situation is one of choice; the other 45% say it has resulted from necessity.

Table 5.13. Willingness to Look After Parents

Nationally	**89%**
Ontario	91
Prairies	88
Quebec	88
BC	87
Atlantic	79
Males	91
Females	86
18-34	90
35-54	88
55+	85
Never Mar	90
Married	88
Cohabiting	88
Div-Sep	88
Widowed	83
Single career	92
Dual career	90
Raised:	
mother & father	89
mother only	86
other	83
Weekly+	92
<Weekly	88

Intergenerational Confessions, Interaction Consequences

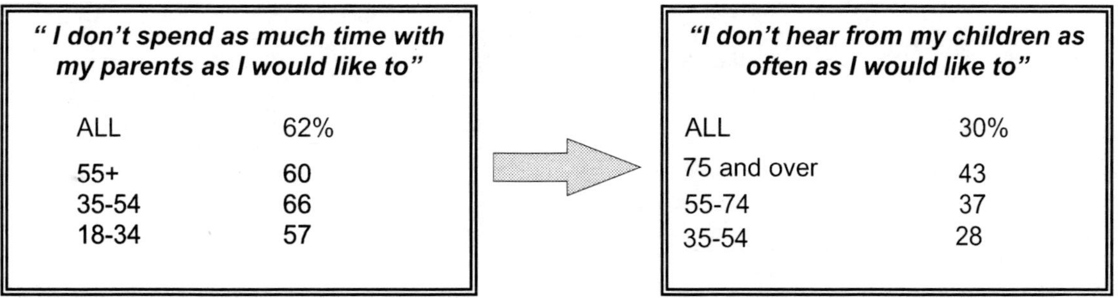

"I don't spend as much time with my parents as I would like to"

ALL	62%
55+	60
35-54	66
18-34	57

"I don't hear from my children as often as I would like to"

ALL	30%
75 and over	43
55-74	37
35-54	28

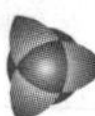

How's Everybody Doing?

As Canadians with children reflect on their ties with their children, almost 80% say that, on balance, they have experienced or are experiencing high levels of enjoyment and very little strain. Most of the rest also say they are receiving quite a bit of enjoyment, but acknowledge that the cost has been quite a bit of strain.

- *Grandparents*, who "are happy to see the kids come and happy to see them go," are more likely than parents to express enjoyment and less likely to report strain. However, about 7% indicate that their grandchildren are a source of considerable stress.[31]

- Nearly 80% of *Canadians with grandparents* say the enjoyment is high and the strain very low. Another 10% or so say the joy is accompanied by a lot strain, perhaps in part because of health problems of many grandmothers and grandfathers. The remaining 10% seem to have limited ties with their grandparents that translate into limited enjoyment and limited strain.

Parents whose children are preschoolers by far enjoy the highest level of enjoyment and lowest level of strain.

- *When "kids" start school*, strain begins to triple what it was in the preschool years. However, contrary to widespread stereotypes, the enjoyment-strain balance remains about the same through *the teen years*.

- Enjoyment levels tend to go up somewhat when children reach their *twenties and beyond*, and strain goes down. However, stress levels are still about twice what they were during the preschool years.

- Parents whose children have *special needs* have joy tempered by strain.

- Mothers who are *employed full-time* claim somewhat higher levels of enjoyment and less strain than mothers who are not employed outside the home.

Table 5.14. Enjoyment and Strain Associated With Children, Grandchildren and Grandparents by Select Variables

"On balance, how much ENJOYMENT and how much STRAIN would you say you experience/or experienced with…"

	Lots/Quite a Bit Enjoyment, Very Little Strain	Quite a Bit Enjoyment, Quite Bit Strain	Not Very Much Enjoyment, Very Little Strain	Not Very Much Enjoyment, Quite Bit Strain	TOTALS
Your children	79%	20	<1	1	100
Your grandchildren	90	5	3	2	100
Your grandparents	79	9	10	2	100
Children					
Preschool age only	91%	9	0	0	100
6-12 only	73	26	0	1	100
13-19 only	71	27	2	0	100
20-plus only	81	18	<1	1	100
No special needs	81	18	<1	<1	100
Have special needs	58	39	1	2	100
Mothers of school-age children					
Employed full-time	76	23	1	0	100
Not employed outside home	64	36	0	0	100

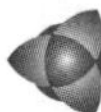

As we might expect, a key factor in predicting the amount of enjoyment versus strain that Canadians experience with their parents is health.

- In cases where their parents do not require care, over 70% of Canadians say they receive high levels of enjoyment from their mothers and their fathers, with very little strain. Things are by no means perfect: for most of the remaining 30%, enjoyment is combined with strain.

- In situations where care is required, enjoyment goes down and strain goes up. Mothers who need care show signs of requiring more than fathers: 24% of adults say their enjoyment of mothers is accompanied by quite a bit of strain, compared to 16% in the case of their fathers.

Table 5.15. Enjoyment and Strain Associated With Children by Children's Age, Health, & Mothers' Employment Status

"On balance, how much ENJOYMENT and how much STRAIN would you say you experience/or experienced with…"

	Lots/Quite a Bit Enjoyment, Very Little Strain	Quite a Bit Enjoyment, Quite Bit Strain	Not Very Much Enjoyment, Very Little Strain	Not Very Much Enjoyment, Quite Bit Strain	TOTALS
Your Mother: *No care required*	71%	20	4	5	100
Care required	58	24	7	11	100
Your Father: *No care required*	68	17	5	10	100
Care required	62	16	9	13	100

THE LONGER LOOK

Parents With School-Age Children

Percentage of the Canadian Population		**1975**	**2000**
One parent employed full-time, one not		29%	14
Two parents employed full-time		7	14
Single mother employed full-time		2	3
Never seem to have enough time		**1985**	**2000**
One parent employed full-time, one not	*Women*	56%	61
[Regardless of who is employed.]	*Men*	46	51
Two parents employed full-time	*Women*	53	61
	Men	57	48
Single mother employed full-time		65	78

Source: Reginald W. Bibby, Project Canada Survey Series.

Summary Note

Approximately 85% of Canadians were raised by their biological parents. Almost all maintain that their parents did a good job of raising them, with such sentiments somewhat higher among those who were raised by their mother and father, followed by those raised by their mother alone. Nine in ten found that home was a safe place, and seven in ten reported high levels of enjoyment and limited strain with their mothers, fathers and siblings.

Canadians are almost unanimous in claiming that they themselves are good parents, including those who are employed outside the home. However, solid majorities of both women and men who are employed full-time say they would stay home and raise their children if they could afford to do so. Even larger majorities indicate that, if they could afford it, they would work part-time and raise their children. Here they are joined by some 70% of "stay-at-home" mothers. People employed outside the home—especially women—express concerns about the lack of time and frequently, the lack of help with household duties; the latter is a complaint of mothers more generally. Time and support issues are particularly serious for divorced women who are employed.

Nine in 10 Canadians—led by older adults— feel that one parent should stay home and look after preschool children in particular. The majority feel that either parent can play this primary child-raising role, but many older adults believe that this role is best filled by mothers. To the extent that child care is required, the preference order of care-givers is partners, parents, other relatives, home-based child care and child care centres. On the topic of spanking, modest majorities favour both keeping it legal and seeing it discouraged.

Regarding some additional parenting issues, seven in ten think that single parents as a whole do a good job raising children. About six in ten think that gay couples can be good parents, and five in ten feel gays and lesbians should be allowed to adopt children. Most support the use of new technologies that enable women to become pregnant. However, just one in twenty think human cloning should be permissible.

Large numbers of older adults whose parents are still living face the reality of their parents requiring care that increasingly requires their time and sometimes their money. While a slight majority of aging parents live in their own dwellings, many have to live elsewhere. Significantly, 89% of Canadians say they would be willing to look after their parents if they need them to do so—something that about 5% are currently doing.

On balance, Canadians receive considerable enjoyment from their children, parents and grandchildren. Yet the findings point to considerable room for relational enhancement. The data show us that both children and parents are enjoyed most when they are young and healthy, and require less from us. Those kinds of realities put a lot of pressure on all children as they get older, on children who have special needs and on parents who are moving into the later phases of their lives. They also are realities that call for much-improved individual and societal responses.

Reflections: How Canadians View Parenthood

It's somewhat amazing how positive Canadians are about how their parents raised them. For all the apparent ups and downs people experienced before leaving home, 95% say that, all things considered, their parents did a good job of bringing them up, including 91% of the growing number who were raised by their mothers. Most people say that home was a safe place. However, the importance of the presence of at least one parent is underlined by another finding—that such a sense of safety was missing for one in four children who were not raised by at least one of their parents.

If Canadians are generous in assessing their parents' performance, they are even more generous in assessing themselves as mothers and fathers. An astounding 99% maintain that they did or are doing a good job of raising their own children. More than eight in ten moms and dads who are employed full-time think they have found a pretty good balance between their jobs and their children. Yet all is not as perfect as the 99% figure would imply. Three in ten of those employed mothers and four in ten fathers admit that their children probably don't think they are spending enough time with them. In the case of employed married and cohabiting mothers, the reason is simple: almost 80% say they never seem to have enough time, in many instances because—idealism aside—household work and the raising of children are not being shared equally by their male partners.

In a perfect world where money was not an issue, most Canadian parents—both female and male—say they would at most work part-time rather than full-time. A sceptic might rightfully suggest that most people—with or without children—would be more than happy to stay home if someone else paid the bills. What seems to be important here, however, is that most mothers and fathers are working outside the home because of financial necessity. The fact of the matter is that 90% believe that it is preferable for one parent to stay home and take primary responsibility for raising children when they are pre-schoolers. But in many cases, that's an impossible dream.

Confronted as they are by the financial realities of family life today, many Canadians see the establishment of child care settings as necessary. The survey shows that child care settings—whether home- or centre-based—are not the top choices of most Canadian parents. If employed parents could have a choice of caregiver for their children, their number one selection would be their partner, followed secondly by one of their parents, and third by another relative.

The survey offers mixed results about parenting by the country's gays and lesbians. Although slightly less than one in two Canadians approve of same sex marriages or of adoption by homosexual men and women, a majority (61%) feel same sex couples can do a good job of raising children—with the figure rising to 74% for adults under 35 years of age. The obvious question that arises is: Why would gays and lesbians be denied the opportunity to adopt if a majority of Canadians think they can be good parents?

Parents begin by caring for their children and very often, in later years, require care from their children. The survey findings concerning aging parents confirm what demographers have been telling us for years. The needs of elderly Canadians are extensive and are only going to be more evident as this segment of the population increases with the aging of baby boomers. Fully nine in ten people say that they would be willing to look after their parents "if they needed me to do so." This may be an extremely important finding, suggesting that solutions may, in part, be found by tapping into the willingness of children to provide care for their parents. But if this sentiment is to serve as a resource in solving the "elder care crisis," the children of these aging parents will need tangible support from the rest of us.

Some Issues Raised by the Findings

1. Many fathers appear to fall short of their self-proclaimed ideals of sharing equally in raising children and looking after household tasks, in the process adding considerable strain to their female partners. What can be done about it?

2. To the extent that child care is necessary to support dual-earner families and lone-parents, is it also possible to provide more financial support and acknowledgment generally to families raising young children so that they have more options? Is it possible to support those parents who rely upon a grandparent or another relative to care for their children part of the time?

3. What are some of the tangible ways in which the willingness of offspring to look after their aging parents can be tapped and supported?

When Relationships End

The survey gave a fair amount of attention to divorce and its impact on Canadians. With the easing of divorce laws in the 1960s and thereafter, divorce in Canada, accelerated during the last part of the century. The Project Canada national survey findings show a steady increase in the proportion of Canadians who have divorced since the mid-1970s, from 7% in 1975 to a current level of 17%.[32]

The reality of divorce has, of course, extensive ramifications. It touches the couple involved as well as children, grandparents and friends, and institutions including schools, the workplace, the media and churches. The increase in divorce has led to important questions concerning the implications for individuals, groups and Canadian society as a whole.

Figure 6.1. Ever-Divorced Canadians: 1975-2003

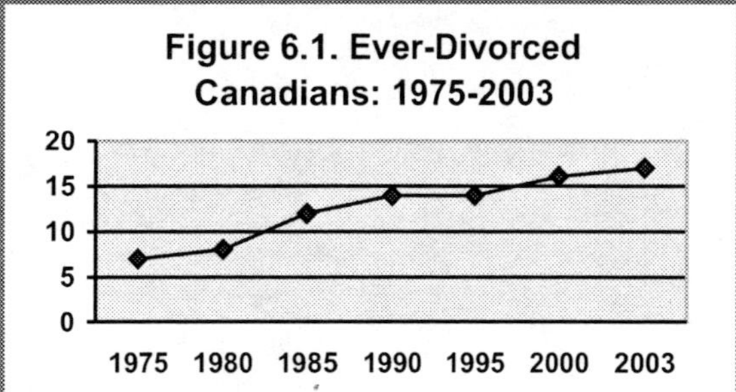

People Who Divorce

Nineteen per cent of our respondents indicated that they have been either divorced or separated at some point in their lives. So had 10% of their parents.

- About 1 in 4 adults who currently live in BC and 1 in 5 who live in *Quebec* and *Ontario* say they have been divorced or separated. The figures are slightly lower for those now living on the *Prairies* and lowest for those in the *Atlantic* region (13%).

- *Females* are somewhat more likely than *males* to acknowledge having had a marriage dissolve.

- *Younger adults*, predictably, have experienced less divorce and separation than others; however, far more grew up with parents who were not together.

- About 3 in 10 individuals who are *cohabiting* have had marriages end, compared to about 1 in 10 people who are *currently married* or *widowed*. Cohabitants also are more likely than others to have had parents who divorced or separated.

- Marital dissolution is only slightly higher among those whose biological *parents were not together* than those whose were.

- The tendency for respondents or their parents to not have lasting marriages differs little by *religion*, with one exception: parents with no declared religion were slightly less likely to have stayed together.

Table 6.1. Divorce & Separation: Respondents & Parents

	Ever Div or Sep	Parents Div or Sep
Nationally	**19%**	**10**
BC	24	12
Quebec	20	13
Ontario	19	8
Prairies	17	10
Atlantic	13	7
Females	23	11
Males	16	8
35-54	25	8
55+	22	5
18-34	7	18
Cohabiting	27	19
Never Married	---	12
Married	12	8
Div-Sep	---	10
Widowed	10	4
At age 16 parents:		
Not together	20	---
Together	19	---
Mothers Religion:		
Roman Catholic	18	11
Protestant	16	8
Other Faith	21	6
None	17	18

We asked Canadians who have been divorced if, as they look back, they thought there was one main reasons for the break-up. Responses were open-ended.

The reflections offered were extremely varied. However, *five primary themes* were evident.

- Foremost was the sense that partners were *going in different directions* regarding values, interests and goals.

- The second most commonly cited factor was *abuse* that took physical, psychological and emotional forms.

- *Alcohol problems* and, to a lesser extent, *drug use*, constituted an important third factor.

- *Infidelity* was the fourth most commonly cited reason for marital breakdown. Despite the prominence this factor is perceived to have, clearly it is a correlate but not necessarily the main source for many people.

- The fifth most frequently cited reason for break-up was *conflict relating to careers*, including issues such as competition, excessive time demands and pressure to make geographical moves.

Table 6.2. The Top Five Reasons for Marital Break-up

1. Different values & interests
2. Abuse: physical, emotional
3. Alcohol & drugs
4. Infidelity
5. Career-related conflict

Quite obviously, divorce is not something to which Canadians aspire. As we saw in section three, almost all Canadians say that, ideally, marriage should last a lifetime, most as teenagers expected to stay with the same partner for life, and even more say they expect their current marriage or relationship to last that long—even if it's the second or third time around. Divorce just happens.

Implications for Individuals

Roughly 80% of Canadians who have experienced divorce or separation acknowledge that the experience was hard on them emotionally, and almost the same proportion says it had a similar effect on their children. Just over one-half indicate that they felt it was hard on their parents.

- In each of these three instances, *females* are more likely than *males* to report negative effects from their break-ups.

- Age-wise, Gen-Xers are somewhat less inclined than older adults to say that their children had difficulty adjusting, but they are slightly more likely to disclose that the split was hard on their parents.

Table 6.3. Marriage Aspirations

% Indicating Strongly Agree or Agree

	Nationally	Ever-Divorced		Parents Div		18-34	35-54	55+
		Yes	No	Yes	No			
Ideally, marriage should last a lifetime	95%	92	96	95	96	96	95	96
As a teenager, I expected to stay same partner for life	82	88	80	76	83	69	83	93
I expect my marriage/relationship to last rest of my life	91	84	93	87	92	88	92	94

"Looking back, was there ONE main reason for the break-up? Would you care to indicate what you think it was?"

Some Response Examples

...we didn't spend enough time together...financial pressures...disinterest...my husband left me...alcohol abuse...spouse's work...another woman...cheating...violence...different values on relationship...I realized I am happier alone...the internet...we both were so immature...dishonesty...drugs...I chose the wrong person...mental cruelty...I grew up in an alcoholic home...he had an affair...abusive partner...my mother-in-law...lying...drinking.. unfaithful...misunderstanding...acted more like a child than a partner...we didn't talk enough...psychological and verbal violence...husband was gone too much...living apart...incompatible...expectations and goals were unrealistic...too much competition...different interests...partner's excessive use of drugs and alcohol...too much change, no stability...infidelity on his part...I was like a piece of luggage as he accepted different opportunities in different locales...adultery...incompatibility of character...not enough time together...emotional abuse...lack of commitment...his alcoholism...my partner met someone else...we grew apart... spouse gambled...money...she did not know what love was all about...he didn't care for the kids...lack of communication...living in a disorderly, unstable society...we were too young...the birth of a child we were told we would not have was too much for him...physical and mental abuse...the booze...abuse and neglect...we didn't know who we were or what we wanted...

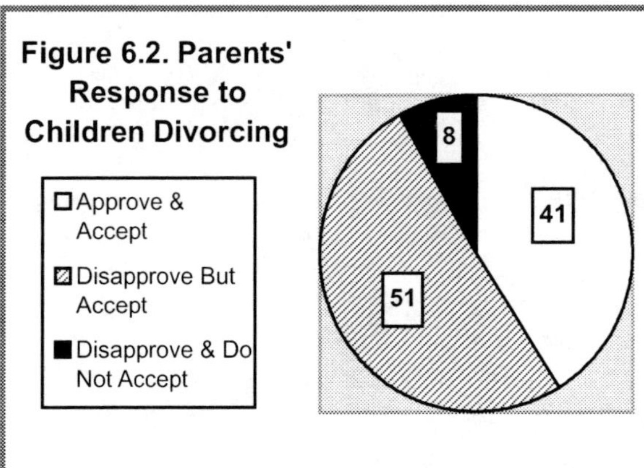

Asked how they feel—or did or would feel—about their children getting a divorce, over 4 in 10 people say they would approve and accept it, while another 5 in 10 would disapprove but being willing to accept. The remainder say they would neither approve nor accept their children divorcing. Approval and acceptance is higher among Gen-Xers (53%) than Boomers (40%) or Pre-Boomers (31%), as well as among people who are not highly involved in religious groups (50%) versus weekly religious service attendees (19%).

About 2 in 3 people say that their divorce or separation was hard on them financially, while close to 1 in 2 say it affected their performance at work.

- In both instances more *females* than *males* report negative effects—particularly in the case of finances.[33] Differences by *age*, however, are small.

- Surprisingly, 80% of the women who ***received child*** *support payments* and received them on time said the divorce or separation was hard on them financially, compared to just 69% of those who either didn't receive support payments or didn't receive them on time. Why? Maybe those who received payments needed the money more and worked harder to get it. Perhaps it reflects relative deprivation: higher income couples are more inclined to make and receive child payments, but—in at least the mother's case—they have to make do with less. We'll return to this issue later.

Table 6.4. Dealing With Divorce and Separation

"How well do the following describe you?"

% Indicating "Very Well" or "Fairly Well"

	Nationally	Females	Males	18-34	35-54	55+
The divorce/separation was hard on me emotionally	80%	84	73	75	82	77
The divorce/separation was hard on my children	76	77	73	69	76	76
The divorce/separation was hard on my parents	54	61	44	63	53	53
The divorce/separation was hard on me financially	65	72	54	70	65	64
The divorce/separation affected my performance at work	46	49	43	45	47	46
I made or received child support payments	50	46	56	44	53	46
I made or received child support payments on time	47	42	56	33	46	54

Child Support Payments: Two Versions

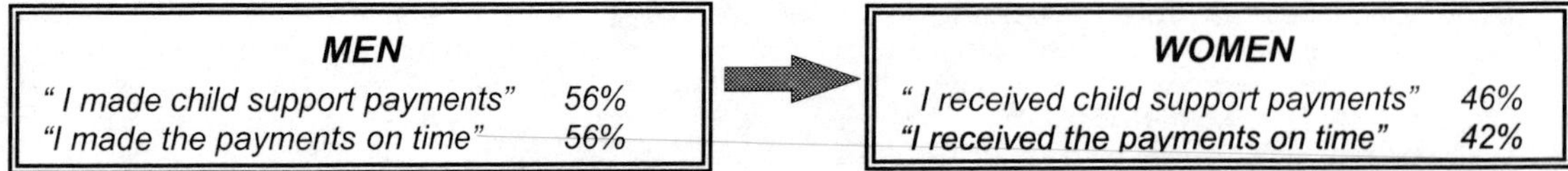

MEN
" I made child support payments" 56%
"I made the payments on time" 56%
WOMEN
" I received child support payments" 46%
"I received the payments on time" 42%

Close to 9 in 10 Canadians who have gone through a divorce or separation say that, all in all, they are happier now than they were when they were in their marriages—and previous marriages, as we have seen, in about 10% of cases. Reflecting on things from this point in time, more than 70% think that their break-ups were "unfortunate but absolutely necessary." Another 18%, however, say that if they "could do it all again, I would have stayed with my partner."

More females than males express positive feelings about the divorce or separation: 23% of men, for example, acknowledge that if they could do it all again they would stay with their wives—a sentiment expressed by only 14% of women.

Younger adults are more likely than their older counterparts both to feel the end of their relationship was necessary and to have no regrets.

Almost all divorced or separated parents—especially mothers—feel that they have achieved a good relationship with their children. Younger parents are slightly less likely to make that claim, at least so far. **One in two further maintain they have been able to achieve a good relationship with their former partners**, with no significant differences either between women and men or among age cohorts.

Has the experience of divorce and separation made relationships less appealing and made individuals feel that they have been negatively labelled?

- About 60% who have gone through such break-ups say they *hesitated to marry or cohabit* again, and 30% say the experience was *stigmatizing*.

- Caution and self-consciousness are more prevalent among *females* than *males*, and also more common among *younger adults* than others.

Table 6.5. The Aftermath of Divorce and Separation

"How well do the following describe you?"

% Indicating "Very Well" or "Fairly Well"

	Nationally	Females	Males	18-34	35-54	55+
All in all, I am happier now than I was when I was in my marriage	87%	92	79	82	85	92
The divorce/separation was unfortunate, but absolutely necessary	73	77	66	89	71	71
If I could do it all again, I would have stayed with my partner	18	14	23	7	19	19
I have been able to achieve a good relationship with my children	94	97	88	84	94	97
I have been able to achieve good relationship with my former spouse	47	47	48	45	48	47
I have/had hesitated to get married or to live together again	58	63	51	65	59	53
I do feel somewhat stigmatized because I am divorced/separated	30	35	22	37	27	31

In short, more women than men express the sense that divorce was necessary but that life has moved on for the better. Younger adults, while **more inclined than others to emphasize the necessity of divorce,** also seem **more likely to still be adjusting** in terms of their **self-image** and **new commitments**.

Implications for Children

Apart from parents, how have Canadian children handled divorce?

As discussed previously in this section, about 10% of adults say that their parents were divorced or separated by the time they were sixteen years old. We asked those now-adult children a number of questions about their experiences.

In the survey, we began with a general statement about the impact of divorce/separation on their lives, and then moved on to some specifics.

- Two-thirds said the marital break-up made *"life harder for us."* More than one-half indicated that a consequence was that "we didn't have enough *money*."

- With respect to *self-esteem*, almost one-half said that they sometimes had "felt inferior to kids whose parents were together," and one-third acknowledged that they sometimes had felt embarrassed by their parents' situation.

- Just over one-third said that the divorce or separation had affected their performance at *school*, with close to one in five adding that it had kept them from *going on* with their education.

- *Relationally*, one-third report that the marital experience of their parents has had a negative effect on their own relationships, but approximately 80% say it has made them "all the more determined to have a lasting relationship."

Table 6.6. Implications for Children

"How well do the following describe you?"

% Indicating "Very Well" or "Fairly Well"

	Nationally	Females	Males	18-34	35-54	55+
Life was harder for us because of my parents' divorce/separation	68%	62	76	69	66	69
As a result of the divorce/separation, we didn't have enough money	58	48	71	51	60	78
I sometimes felt inferior to kids whose parents were together	45	39	53	39	51	52
The divorce/separation affected my performance at school	36	28	49	31	42	41
I sometimes felt embarrassed by my parents' situation	37	33	43	25	45	64
The divorce/separation kept me from going on with my education	17	18	15	7	24	42
I have been all the more determined to have a lasting relationship	79	74	85	78	79	76
I find it has had a negative effect on my own relationships	34	33	36	26	44	37

Some important variations exist by both gender and age.

- *Males* are consistently more likely than *females* to speak of their parents' divorce or separation as having had negative effects on their lives—with the sole exception of being less likely to think it stood in the way of their going on with school.

- Perhaps reflecting both the greater prevalence and acceptance of divorce in recent decades, *Gen-Xers* under 35 are consistently less likely than *Boomers* and *Boomers' parents* to indicate that the end of their parents' relationship had negative effects on their lives. However, the differences are relative: 69% of Gen-Xers say that they *did* find that life became harder, while significant numbers found it affected their self-esteem, school performance and relationships.

And how did everybody turn out?

Today, people who came from homes where their parents were together are somewhat more likely than those who divorced or separated to say that:

- all things considered, they are "very happy"
- relationally they are likewise "very happy" with their partners
- financially, they are "pretty well satisfied"
- they have been to university.

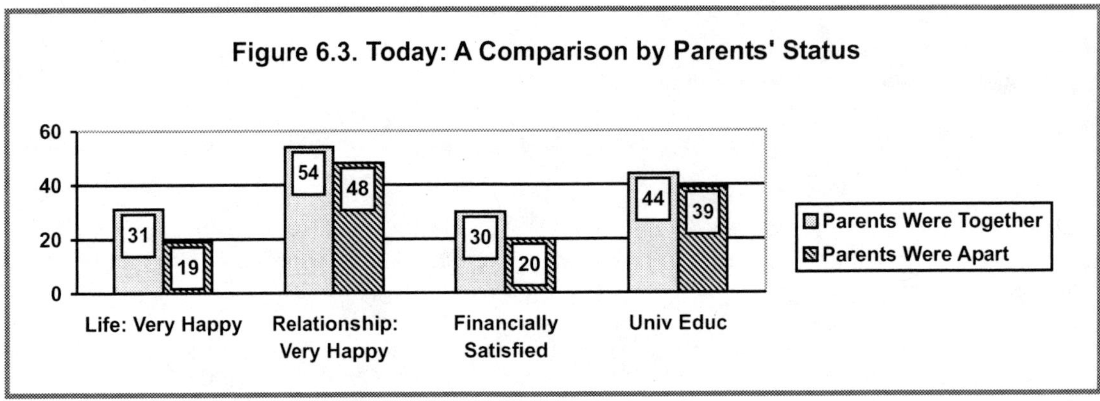

An examination by age further suggests that growing up with divorce continues to take a toll in adulthood, especially in the early adult years.

- The differences noted above persist regardless of whether we are looking at Pre-Boomers, Boomers, or Gen-Xers. Within each cohort, people who grew up with their parents together are consistently more likely than those who did not to report higher levels of happiness, financial satisfaction and education.

- If anything, *the differences are greater* for 18- to 34-year-olds than older adults—suggesting that the effects of their parents not being together persist.

Table 6.7. Characteristics Today by Parents' Status

	Life: V Happy	Relship V Happy	Finan Sat	Univ Educ
18-34				
Parents together	35%	68	28	53
Parents not together	18	54	20	39
35-54				
Parents together	27	52	27	44
Parents not together	17	42	17	45
55+				
Parents together	32	49	34	38
Parents not together	27	48	23	27

Is there a positive finding in all this? The differences—even in the case of education—may well tend to diminish as people get older. **Growing up in a home where parents are together seems to provide an emotional and financial head start. But many people from homes that were not intact nonetheless eventually achieve those goals as well.** The downside is that they appear to have to work harder to achieve the same happy endings.

Implications for Starting Over

To discover the experience that Canadians have had with remarriage, we asked our survey participants, *"Have you ever remarried or had a partner who was previously married?"* The item attempted to identify people who explicitly have remarried, while at the same time expanding the category to include individuals who have been or are in a relationship with someone who was previously married. Consequently the item looks at life history, not just present circumstances.

In response to the query, 17% of our survey participants said, "Yes." [34]

- About 4 in 10 of the 17% told us that they have been *married two or more times*.

- Another 4 in 10 said they have been married once—and now have or in the past had a partner who was previously married.

- The remaining 2 in 10 have *never been married* themselves but have had or now have partners who at one time were married.

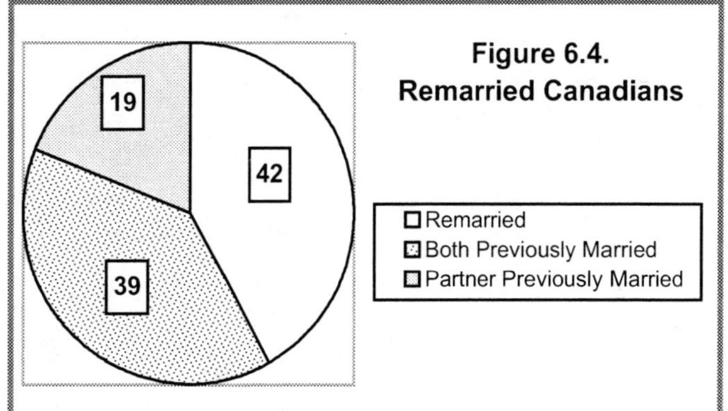

Figure 6.4. Remarried Canadians

Remarriage or cohabitation with a person who was previously married is:

- proportionally most prevalent among people who currently are living in *British Columbia* and the least common among individuals residing in the *Atlantic region*

- equally common among *females* and *males*

- reported more often by adults who now are *35 and older* than by *younger adults*

- slightly more likely among people who have come from homes in which their own *parents were not together* versus intact homes

- somewhat more common among *Protestants* than *Catholics* and adherents to *Other World Faiths*; the "no religion" figure is appreciable (15%) given that, in the population as a whole, a disproportionate number of young adults are in the "None" category.

Table 6.8. Remarried Canadians

"Have you ever remarried or had a partner who was previously married?"

Nationally	**17%**
BC	24
Ontario	16
Quebec	14
Prairies	18
Atlantic	10
Females	17
Males	16
35-54	22
55+	19
18-34	7
At age 16 parents:	
Together	16
Not together	19
Mother's Religion:	
Protestant	18
None	15
Roman Catholic	13
Other World Faith	11

We asked people who had entered into remarriages about the quality of the ties with their new partners and, where applicable, the children involved. In cases where people had more than one new spouse or partner over time, we asked them to generalize.

Almost 8 in 10 report their new relationships as being much happier than their earlier ones.

- Most positive are *males* and *people who remarried*.

- The least positive about the new ties are *never-married* individuals who are involved with someone who was *previously married.*

More than 8 in 10 people maintain that (1) they adjusted "very well" or "fairly well" to their partners' children, and that (2) their partners' children adjusted well to them.[35]

• The sense that they adjusted well to their partners' children is held equally by *females* and *males*. However, males are slightly more inclined than females to feel their partners' children adjusted well to them.

• In both adjustment instances, *individuals who remarried*—while reporting a good adjustment (about 75%)—are somewhat less likely to adjust than individuals who entered new relationships but *did not or have not remarried*.

Almost the same level of 8 in 10 people reported that in cases in which both partners had children, the children involved "adjusted well to each other." Differences by gender are fairly small (females 80%, males 73%), and are insignificant between those who remarried and those who married someone who previously was married.

Table 6.9. Remarriage and New Relationship Adjustments

"How well do the following describe you?""

% Indicating "Very Well" or "Fairly Well"

	Nationally	Females	Males	Remar	Both Prev Mar	Partner Prev Mar
My subsequent relationship was much happier than my first	78%	74	81	83	75	68
I adjusted well to my partner's children	83	84	82	75	89	84
My partner's children adjusted well to me	79	75	82	73	84	79
My children & my partner's children adjusted well to each other	76	80	73	81	78	***

*Insufficient number of cases to permit stable percentaging or generalizing.

Thinking back on their experiences in stepfamilies when they were growing up, 56% of Canadians say they got along well with their stepparents and 65% say the same thing about their stepsiblings.

• There are no differences by *gender* in either case.

• However, in such family situations, *Gen-Xers* and *Boomers* are slightly more likely than *Pre-Boomers* to report positive experiences: slightly more say they got along well with their stepfathers and stepmothers, and far more indicate they had positive ties with their stepbrothers and stepsisters.

Table 6.10. Interpersonal Relations in Blended Families

"How well do the following describe you?"

% Indicating "Very Well" or "Fairly Well"

" I got along well with my..."	Nationally	Females	Males	18-34	35-54	55+
stepfather/stepmother	56%	57	55	56	58	50
stepbrother(s)/stepsister(s)	65	66	63	65	73	41

Comparing levels of enjoyment and strain in stepfamilies with all Canadian families at this point in time is potentially illuminating. Unlike the above item that probes childhood experiences, the survey also asked about *current relations* with stepfamily members. This has the advantage of both monitoring stepfamily relations into adulthood and providing information on people who, as adults "came to have stepparents and stepsiblings" when their parents remarried.

The general patterns are fairly clear.

• In the case of *stepfamilies*, biological mothers have slightly higher enjoyment levels and less strain than stepparents and biological fathers—who share similar enjoyment-strain levels. With siblings, the differences are also fairly small, but enjoyment is somewhat higher among biological brothers and sisters than stepsiblings.

• When stepfamily relations are compared with those of *Canadian families more generally,* the enjoyment/strain levels of biological mothers and siblings are virtually identical. Slightly lower is the gratification received from biological fathers who, in the case of divorce and remarriage, typically were replaced structurally by stepfathers.

Table 6.11. Adults Experiences of Enjoyment and Strain: Stepfamilies and All Families

"On balance, how much ENJOYMENT and how much STRAIN would you say you experience/or experienced with..."

	Lots/Quite a Bit Enjoyment, Very Little Strain	Quite a Bit Enjoyment, Quite Bit Strain	Not Very Much Enjoyment, Very Little Strain	Not Very Much Enjoyment, Quite Bit Strain	TOTALS
Stepfamilies					
Your biological mother	68%	17	8	7	100
Your biological father	61	19	9	11	100
Your stepmother/father	60	17	12	11	100
Your biological brother(s)/sister(s)	69	20	9	2	100
Your stepbrother(s)/stepsister(s)	61	10	15	14	100
All Families					
Your mother	70	20	4	6	100
Your father	67	17	6	10	100
Your brother(s)/sister(s)	69	18	8	5	100

Is There Anything That Can Be Done?

Earlier we made the point that Canadians do not aspire to have relationships that end. The vast majority hope for lasting ties from the time they are young. When their initial relationships don't last, most don't give up. On the contrary, they enter into new ones and intend to have them last.

In light of such goals and dreams, we asked Canadians, ***"What do you think that we, as a society, might do in order to help people have happy and lasting marriages?"*** We asked for an assessment of seven possibilities, and gave respondents the opportunity to offer any further suggestions.

- More than 90% agree that *more counselling* is needed to help people cope with their problems, along with *more information* generally to help people with their marriages.

- About 1 in 3 think it should be *more difficult* for people to get divorced, and 1 in 4 think it should be *more difficult* for people *to get married.*

- Close to 80% maintain that it would helpful if marriage courses were provided in our *schools*, while about 70% feel marriages would benefit from more support from the media.

- Perhaps significantly, 1 in 3 agree with the assertion that, *"Frankly, I don't think there is much we can do."*

Maybe it's a comment on our widespread consensus; perhaps it says more about our lack of creativity. Either way, differences in views as to what might enhance marriage—including the limited number of open-ended responses that went beyond premarital counselling (2%)—**vary little** by gender, age and having or having not experienced divorce and separation. The only notable exception is the tendency for older adults to think it should be more difficult for people to get married or divorced, as well as to think more support for marriage should be provided by schools and the media.

Table 6.12. Reflections on How Marriage Might Be Enhanced by Gender, Age, and Marital Experiences

	NAT	Females	Males	18-34	35-54	55+	Ever Sep/Div Yes	Ever Sep/Div No
Provide more counselling help people cope with their problems	93%	94	92	95	91	95	93	93
Provide more information help people with their marriages	90	91	89	90	88	93	89	90
Make it more difficult for people to get divorced	34	33	35	30	32	42	32	34
Make it more difficult for people to get married	27	29	26	23	26	33	34	25
Provide courses on marriage in our schools	78	78	77	67	80	86	84	76
Provide more support for marriage in the media	72	75	70	66	72	80	70	73
Frankly, I don't think there is much we can do	33	33	33	34	31	36	36	32

A quick demographic and social scan of the 30% of Canadians who don't think much can be done "to help people have happy and lasting marriages" reveals some interesting patterns.

- The pessimism or skepticism is *higher in Quebec* than anywhere else; optimism is highest on the Prairies.

- People who have been either *previously married or never married* are less inclined to think much can be done than people who are currently married, including those who have remarried.

- Education is important: those with lower levels of education are less optimistic that marriage can be enhanced.

- Canadians who say they have *"no religion"*—who also are disproportionately young—are considerably more likely than people who identify with Christianity and Other World Faiths to be pessimistic. Beyond sheer identification, people who are actively involved in religious groups tend to be more optimistic that something can be done to help people with their marriages.

Table 6.13. People Pessimistic About the Enhancing of Marriage in Canada

Nationally	**33%**
Quebec	39
Ontario	34
Atlantic	31
BC	30
Prairies	27
Cohabiting	42
Widowed	40
Div-Sep	36
Never Married	36
Remarried	30
Married	29
HS or Less	42
Tech-bus-college	29
Univ Grads	29
None	40
Protestant	32
Roman Catholic	31
Other World Faiths	28
Less Weekly	35
Weeklys	24

Finally, one group that maintains hope that something can be done to help people with married life consists of those individuals who say they expect to stay with the same partners for life. Their expectations are telling.

- More than 70% who strongly believe that *their marriages or relationships will last* for the rest of their lives also think there are societal resources available that can be helpful.

- Conversely, 43% of those who strongly feel that *their relationships will not be permanent* don't think very much can be done to help people have happy and lasting ties.

Figure 6.5. Belief Society Can Help Enhance Marriage by Extent to Which People Expect Their Relationships to Last a Lifetime

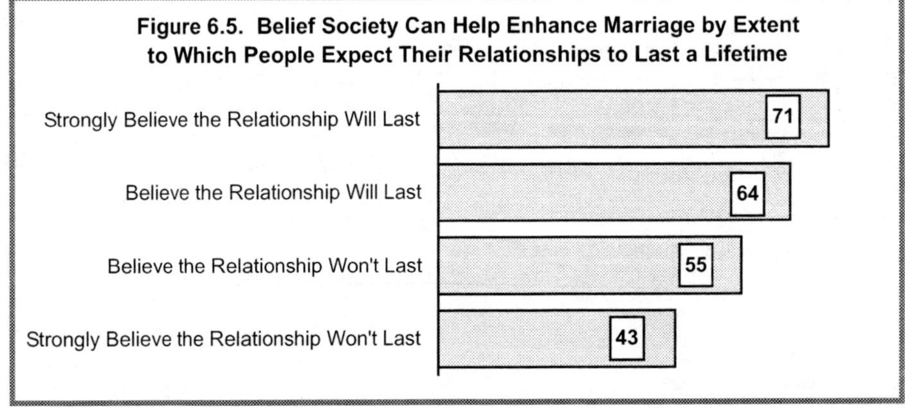

THE LONGER LOOK

Divorce: Select Behaviour and Attitudes: 1980 and 2000

	1980	2000
Ever-divorced Canadians	8%	18
...as a % of all adults who have married	10	22
...% who attend religious services weekly or more	4	11
...% who attend religious services less than weekly	10	17
Divorce should be easier to obtain than it is now	42	34
Family breakdown is a very serious problem in Canada	40	35

Source: Reginald W. Bibby, Project Canada Survey Series.

Summary Note

One in five Canadians has been either divorced or separated at some point in their lives. So were one in ten of their parents. People who divorce do so because they feel it is absolutely necessary, related primarily to issues such as different interests, abuse, alcohol and drugs, infidelity and career-related conflict.

The dissolution of a relationship is emotionally hard on most people, including their children and many parents. Very often, divorce makes life tough financially and makes jobs more difficult to perform. Yet looking back, most see their divorces as necessary. Relatively few—if they could wind back the clock—would do things differently.

Almost all divorced or separated parents, especially mothers, feel they have achieved good ties with their children, and one in two claim the same about their relationships with their former partners. A majority feel the experience has resulted in their being hesitant to marry or cohabit again, and about one in three feel stigmatized. Younger adults are often still dealing with self-image and commitment issues.

Adults whose parents did not stay together—particularly males—frequently report that life was harder on them, having negative impacts on finances, self-image and, in some cases, performance at school and continuing their education. While some feel the experience of their parents had a negative effect on their own relationships, about 80% say it strengthened their resolve to have lasting relationships. The possible legacy of divorce and separation is suggested by the finding that people from homes where their parents stayed together claim somewhat higher levels of happiness, financial satisfaction and educational attainment than others. Differences are particularly apparent in the early adult years; however, these differences tend to dissipate over time.

People might separate and divorce, but few give up on relationships. About one in five Canadians are in relationships that involve previously married individuals. Most say their new ties are much happier than their earlier ones, and that—where children have been involved—everyone has adjusted reasonably well. For the most part, such claims are corroborated by what adults report about their experiences with their stepparents and stepsiblings. Moreover, more than 80% of people with new partners expect their relationships to last the rest of their lives.

A majority of Canadians maintain that society can contribute to people having “happy and lasting marriages” primarily by providing more counselling and more information. Belief that one can have and will have a happy and lasting relationship may have a self-fulfilling effect, in that it is strongly associated with a greater willingness to find ways to make marriage work.

The broader question of how we, as a society, might respond to what Canadians want from family life more generally is the topic of the final section of the report.

Reflections
How Canadians Feel About Divorce and Its Impact

Divorce is not a Canadian aspiration. It is certainly not part of Canadian hopes and dreams. Yet it is a reality that has been experienced by approximately one in four people who have married. That's nowhere near the two in four figure that is widely cited. But it is still relatively high given what couples have in mind on their wedding day and the fact that more than nine in ten people say they expect to stay with their current partner for life, even when their current partner is not their first one.

The frequency of divorce appears to have done little to minimize its impact on everyone involved. It is true that Canadians have been more accepting of divorce, in light of its growing incidence since the 1950s. Indicative of those changing cultural views, younger adults whose parents have divorced report less stigma, fewer problems with self-esteem, and less difficulty with finances and educational aspirations than their older counterparts. They are also less inclined to say that the experience of their parents has dulled their inclination to enter into new relationships.

Yet the differences are relative: the survey shows that, among adults under 35, five in ten say that as a result of their parents' divorce, they didn't have enough money. Four in ten say they felt inferior to kids whose parents were together. Three in ten report the divorce affected their performance at school. Close to the same proportion say the divorce has had a negative effect on their own relationships. And, to be sure, those numbers represent a lot of children.

As for divorcing adults, most acknowledge that divorce has been hard on them emotionally and financially. They also report that their divorce was difficult for their parents and particularly for their children. Close to one in two acknowledge that their performance at work was or is currently being affected.

Remarriage is often a solution but not always. In about one in four cases, people find that their new relationship is not happier than their previous one. In some one in five instances, partners don't adjust particularly well to their partner's children. Not surprisingly, in a similar number of cases, the childrens' feelings are reciprocal.

To the extent that Canadians aspire to have a society in which adults and children experience optimum living, these findings are decisive and the reality needs to be stated clearly: marriages need to be strengthened in order to reduce the proportion that end in divorce. Let's not mince words: these results serve to remind us that divorce carries with it enormous personal, interpersonal, and societal costs. Of course there are a large number of situations where new beginnings are necessary and hopefully life-giving. But now that divorce laws have been liberalized, making it easier for people who require a divorce to be obtain one, more liberal legislation is not what most Canadians want need or want. I'm not exagerating. In 1985, 45% of the nation said, "divorce in this country should be easier to obtain than it is now." As of 2000, the figure had fallen to 34%.

The survey results suggest that what Canadians—young and old—want at this point in our history is to have relationships that last. They aspire to avoid finding themselves in situations that call for divorce. They need some help to realize those dreams.

Some Issues Raised by the Findings

1. Give that Canadians marry with the expectation of a life-long relationship, what are the factors that lead so many to separate and divorce?

2. Given that the large majority of those who divorce say that it was absolutely necessary to end the relationship, should we attempt to reduce the level of divorce?

3. Can marriages be strengthened and the numbers of divorce reduced without such efforts leading to disparaging attitudes and policies toward individuals and families who have experienced divorce?

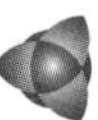

Responding to Family Hopes and Dreams

Beyond trying to clarify what Canadians want from family life, the survey explored some of their thoughts about how their aspirations and hopes might be realized.

Priorities

We asked respondents, ***"How high a priority do you think we should give..."*** to sixteen areas and issues raised in the survey.

In the minds of most Canadians, the top priorities are very clear: health care for people of all ages and income brackets, and *children.*

- The child-related issues pertain to ensuring their health and safety, and include creating *safe environments* at school and at home, and protecting them from abuse and exploitation by dealing with *child pornography*.

- Part of the desire for safe environments at home is expressed in terms of giving high priority to addressing *violence in the home*.

- Concern for children is also expressed in the call for high priority to be given to issues such as supporting parents who have *children with special needs*, and ensuring that *child support payments* are made.

Table 7.1.
The Top Ten Family -Related Priorities
Viewed by 50% or More as Warranting "Very High Priority"

Priority	%
1. **Health care** for Canadians of all ages	80%
2. Safe environments for **children** at school	79
3. Strengthening **child** pornography legislation	75
4. Safe environments for **children** at home	73
5. **Medical care** to families who cannot afford it	70
6. Addressing violence in the home	68
7. Support for parents of **children** with special needs	58
8. Ensuring that **child** support payments are made	53
9. Food and housing for families who cannot afford it	52
10. Helping low income parents resolve employment problems	45
Help for those who care for elderly parents	45

- Rounding out the top priorities—those issues seen as of premier importance by close to half or more of respondents—is ensuring that low income families receive adequate *food and housing* and that parents in such situations receive help in resolving *employment problems*. "Tied for tenth" is a specific health issue: help for people who care for *elderly parents*.

Four of the five other issues put to Canadians are seen by about 1 in 3 as warranting "very high priority":

- *strengthening marriages* to reduce divorce
- helping *low-income parents* resolve their *financial problems*
- *providing child care* for parents *employed outside the home*
- *providing financial support* for *parents who stay at home* with their children.

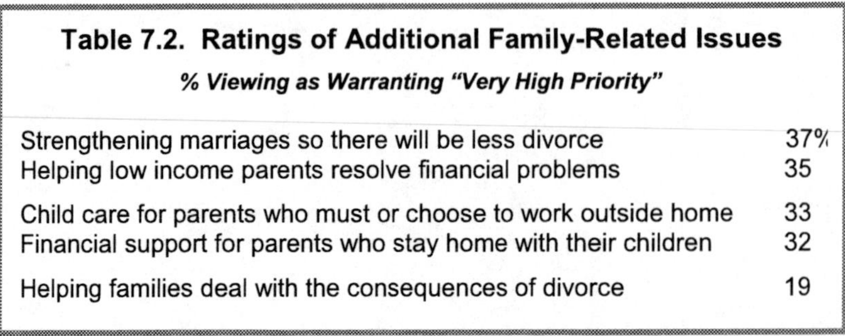

Table 7.2. Ratings of Additional Family-Related Issues

% Viewing as Warranting "Very High Priority"

Strengthening marriages so there will be less divorce	37%
Helping low income parents resolve financial problems	35
Child care for parents who must or choose to work outside home	33
Financial support for parents who stay home with their children	32
Helping families deal with the consequences of divorce	19

A smaller percentage—19%—feel that "very high priority" should be given to helping families deal with the *consequences of divorce*. As noted, almost twice as many people feel the priority should be given to proactively *strengthening marriages* and reducing divorce. Those who have never been divorced or separated are just as likely as those who have to favour strengthening marriages, but are less inclined to give priority to dealing with divorce's consequences.

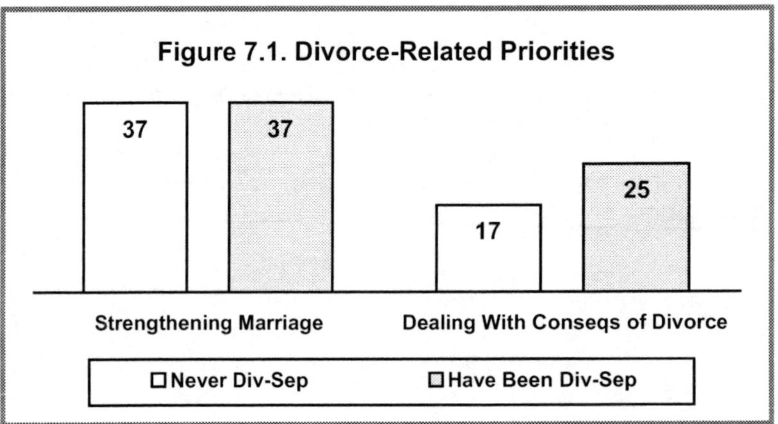

Figure 7.1. Divorce-Related Priorities

In the case of *parenting and employment*, employed parents with children under thirteen almost equally favour resources being made available both to people in their situation (40%) and to parents of young children who stay home (36%). However, mothers of young children are considerably more likely to say their situations should be given higher priority (68%) than child care for people employed outside the home (37%).

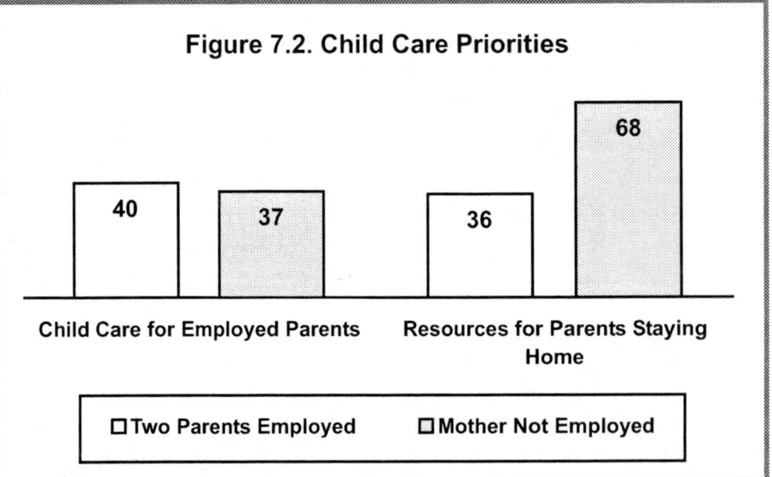

Figure 7.2. Child Care Priorities

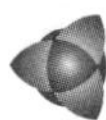

Who Are The Key Players in Raising Children?

In light of the supreme value that is given to children, it's important to clarify who Canadians see as playing the key roles that ensure they are raised well. *We asked our respondents how important fifteen factors are in contributing to "children being raised healthy and happy,"* and gave them the opportunity to cite any other single key source we may have omitted.

In most people's minds, the **two most important sources** for healthy and happy children are parents ***who spend time with them***, and ***feeling that they are loved***. Close behind these two factors is ***positive self-esteem***– children feel good about themselves.

Being loved and self-esteem are closely tied to being "healthy and happy." So the question remains, beyond parents, how do children get there? Here Canadians offer some specifics.

- Some 6 in 10—led by younger adults—see *friends* as an important source of feelings of well-being and worth. Five in 10—led by women and older adults—point to the significance of children *enjoying school*. One assumes they are thinking of school as a total experience that contributes to happiness, good ties and building self-esteem, versus just the academic side of school.

- Under 5 in 10 people point to other family members as key sources of health and happiness—notably *grandparents* who spent time with them and *brothers and sisters*. Not surprisingly, people 55 and over are more enthusiastic about grandparents. So are women.

There are a number of other important players in the minds of many Canadians.

Table 7.3. Key Sources of Children's Well -Being by Gender & Age

"How important do you think these factors are to children being raised healthy and happy?"

% Indicating "Very Important"

	NAT	Women	Men	18-34	35-54	55+
Parents who spend time with them	95%	96	94	95	95	94
Feeling they are loved	95	97	94	95	95	96
Feeling good about themselves	87	90	85	88	87	87
Having some close friends	61	64	58	71	58	56
Enjoying school	51	56	45	46	47	61
Grandparents who spend time with them	46	53	40	43	43	55
Having brothers and sisters	43	42	43	40	41	48

- Some 4 in 10 people say that children's lives will be enriched if they can *enjoy their teachers*. Women and older adults are more inclined than others to emphasize this point. It should not be a surprising assertion, given the amount of time young people spend in school, and the way in which their experiences with teachers colour their lives. And adults know; they have been there.

- About 3 in 10 people see five other factors as being "very important" to healthy and happy children: spending a certain amount of time alone—particularly espoused by women and younger adults—having *other relatives* share in their lives, being involved in *sports* and *other activities*, and growing up with adequate *finances*. Summed up, it works out to a combination of healthy solitude, further social ties and recreational outlets, and enough money to make it all possible.

- About 15% of adults also think that involvement in *religious groups* and *other groups* contributes to children's well-being.

Table 7.4. Additional Sources of Children's Well -Being

"How important do you think these factors are to children being raised healthy and happy?"

% Indicating "Very Important"

	NAT	Women	Men	18-34	35-54	55+
Enjoying their teachers	38	43	33	31	37	48
Spending a certain amount of time alone	34	39	30	45	28	32
Other relatives who share in their lives	32	36	27	36	30	30
Being involved in other activities*	31	33	28	33	30	30
Growing up with adequate finances	30	31	29	30	29	31
Being involved in sports	28	29	28	26	28	30
Being involved in religious groups	16	17	15	14	13	22
Being involved in other groups	14	16	13	15	12	16

*In the questionnaire, this item followed "Being involved in sports."

Some Predictable Correlations

Own Life Experiences		Very Important for Children
Brothers and sisters	→	***To have brothers and sisters***
Lots of enjoyment, little strain		**57%**
Little enjoyment, lots of strain		**34**
Follow sports	→	***To be involved in sports***
Weekly or more		36%
Less than weekly		20
Attend religious services	→	***To be involved in religious groups***
Weekly or more		42%
Less than weekly		6

Who's Responsible for Enhancing Family Life

We've looked at what people want from family life, and, also listened to what they have been saying about the key sources of well-being for their children.

A critical question is who is actually going to take responsibility for enhancing family life? Canadians seem to have some pretty clear ideas as to where the major contributions need to be coming from.

- Almost everyone agrees that the starting point is *parents*.

- As children grow up, *they too* (offspring) have a responsibility. Lest anyone be confused, 84% of adults 55 and over look to children—in many instances their own—to enhance family life. The levels are not that much lower for adults under 55.

- Consistent with what we just saw about the importance of schools and teachers, more than 60% of Canadians say that *schools* also have a major responsibility for enriching family life. Close to the same proportion say the same about *governments*.

- About 1 in 2 people think that good family life requires the help of *other relatives*—siblings, grandparents, aunts, uncles, cousins, and so on. Their responsibility is called for particularly by younger Gen-Xers, who have experienced more separation and divorce than any other previous Canadian generation.

- Approximately 40% maintain that *family agencies*, *religious groups*,[36] *employers* and the *media* need to make significant contributions to family life.[37]

- Around 30% say the same about *neighbourhoods*.

- Somewhat surprisingly, just over 20% feel that the *business sector* has a high level of responsibility for enriching family life.

Table 7.5. Who's Responsible for Enhancing Family Life by Gender and Age

"How much responsibility do you think the following have for enhancing family life?"

% Indicating "A Great Deal" or "**Quite A Bit**"

	NAT	Women	Men	18-34	35-54	55+
Parents	98%	98	98	98	98	98
Children	78	78	78	72	77	84
Schools	63	63	63	66	58	69
Governments	60	61	59	59	62	59
Other relatives	49	52	47	57	46	45
Family Agencies	42	48	36	42	43	41
Religious groups	41	41	41	38	38	51
Employers	40	41	39	35	42	42
The media	36	39	34	36	37	37
Neighbourhoods	31	33	30	30	30	34
The business sector	22	23	22	16	24	26

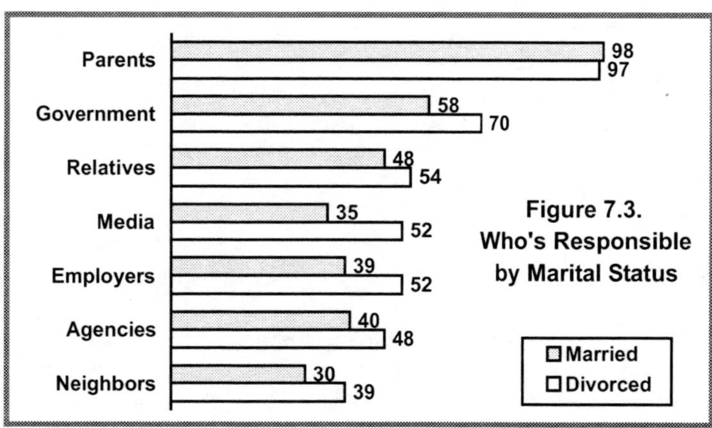

Figure 7.3. Who's Responsible by Marital Status

Differences in required sources are apparent for people who are married versus divorced.

Who's Going to Pay the Bills?

In the final section of the questionnaire, we confronted respondents with the issue of costs. *"Given that resources are needed to enhance family life, who do you think should share the costs"* of six general services: child care, raising children, activities for young people, post-secondary education, information and counselling, and care for the elderly. Governments, families, and communities were posed as possible contributors; in the community instance, "groups" and "fund-raising were offered as examples.

- The dominant sentiment is that *child care costs* should be shared primarily by families and governments. About 1 in 4 people feel that communities also should help out.

- The costs of *raising children,* say most, should be borne foremost by families and to a lesser extent by governments.

- *Activities for young people* are seen as something requiring the financial lead of families and communities, with governments contributing to some extent.

Table 7.6. Who Should Share the Costs of Key Services

	Govts	Families	Communities
Child-care	68%	74	23
Costs of raising children	46	85	12
Activities for young people	40	68	66
Post-secondary education	81	65	15
Information & counselling	68	47	51
Care for the elderly	87	63	39

- The costs of *post-secondary education* are viewed as the responsibility of governments first and families second.

- *Information and counselling* are seen as services in which governments should be financially involved, but the costs —say one in two Canadians—should also be covered by communities and families.

- Of all these areas, the one for which the largest number of people are calling for government support is *care for the elderly* (87%); it even outdistances post-secondary education (81%). At the same time, more than 6 in 10 people say families should contribute to such costs, and 4 in 10 say that communities should also help out financially.

We can safely predict correlations between services needed and the people involved—such as parents with children, university students, individuals who are divorced and people who are older.

The more important point that these findings underline is the relative financial balance people feel is appropriate. Relatively few people expect governments alone to pick up all the bills. On the contrary, it seems significant that there is widespread recognition that some areas require substantial investments on the part of families, and others the financial support of communities.

Who's Providing the Social Capital?

A final note. In the course of trying to better understand what Canadians want from family life beyond what they have been and are currently experiencing, the empirically-based assumption we have been making is that the family unit—however conceptualized and experienced—is of fundamental importance to them.

As individuals struggle to experience a good home life as children, pursue what they hope will be good relationships, and aspire to be good parents and eventually good grandparents, most do so consciously, unconsciously believing that their own well-being is intrinsically linked to their family. That seems to be why, regardless of what happens, "we all keep trying" in the varied family roles we find ourselves playing over a lifetime. Most people want to be known as "a good" daughter or son, husband or wife, partner or companion, grandmother or grandfather.

That which is often elusive is also a source of joy and sustenance—but frequently a source of pain and strain as well. **So as we all pursue enhanced family life, who provides the human resources—the "social capital" that adds to our lives?**[38]

We've looked at some of the relational sources of enjoyment and strain throughout this report. To sum up:

- Nationally, the two major social sources of enjoyment and minimal strain are *grandchildren* and *friends* they offer a lot, maybe in large part because we typically can say goodbye as readily as we say hello. Pets get almost an equally high rating for much the same reason.

- One's *immediate family* tends to form a second tier of enjoyment and strain—children and partners at the top of the tier, siblings and fathers at the bottom. With partners, we are in it for the length of our commitment; with the others—like it or not—we are in it for the long run.

- A *third tier* of social support for most Canadians consists of in-laws, stepfamily members, colleagues at work and neighbours. The latter is important: 57% of our respondents say that neighbours bring them high levels of enjoyment and very little strain. Yet for another 25% of Canadians, neighbours are not well-known and, as such, are seen as neither bringing much enjoyment nor strain (i.e., very little of anything) to their lives.

Table 7.7. Relational Sources of Enjoyment: A Summary

On Balance Experiencing or Experienced High Levels of Enjoyment and Very Little Strain

	Nationally	Women	Men	18-34	35-54	55+
Your grandchildren	90%	87	93	---	86	93
Friends	87	85	88	85	85	91
Your pet(s)	*85*	*86*	*85*	*88*	*81*	*89*
Your grandparents	79	79	80	80	75	87
Your children	79	78	81	86	74	85
Your marriage/relationship	74	67	80	69	73	79
Your mother	70	66	75	69	69	74
Your brother(s)/sisters	69	67	72	73	63	77
Your father	67	64	71	69	65	70
Your in-law(s)	64	58	71	64	62	70
People at work	63	62	64	61	61	69
Your stepbrother(s)/stepsister(s)	61	62	59	65	59	57
Your stepmother/father	60	50	69	53	63	61
Your neighbours	57	58	55	47	52	71

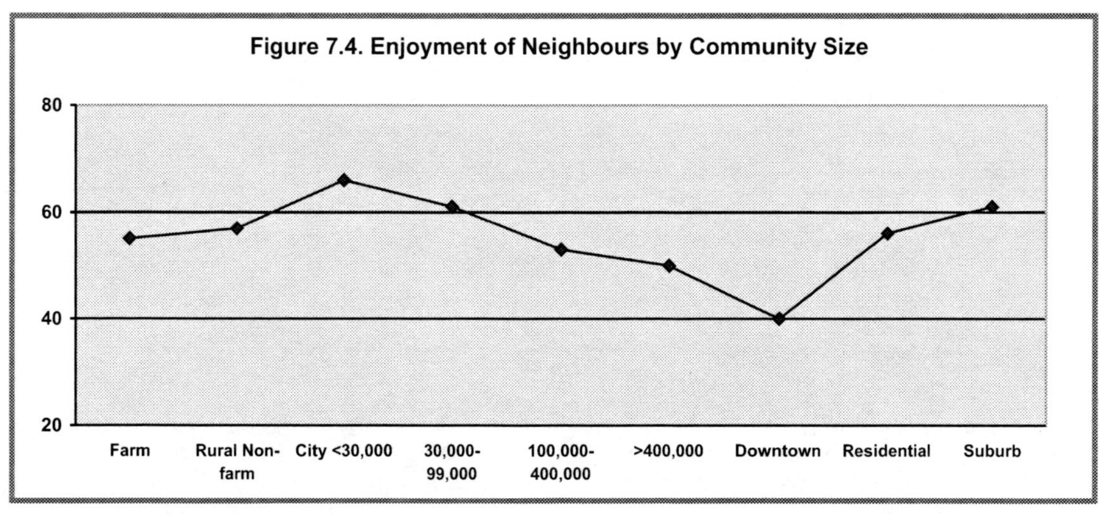

Figure 7.4. Enjoyment of Neighbours by Community Size

The extent to which Canadians receive social support is illustrated by findings concerning how often they engage in a variety of activities with partners, children, friends and other family members—and also the extent to which they pray. Clearly there are considerable variations. But **what is striking is the central role of partners and children in both requiring and providing social resources**. God also seems to warrant a footnote.

Table 7.8. Some Key Social Resources

"Generally speaking, about how often do you find you..."

	Weekly or More	Monthly: or More	Yearly	Never	TOTALS
Eat a meal at home...					
with your partner	95%	2	1	2	100
with your children	72	16	9	3	100
by yourself	67	13	13	7	100
with another family member(s)	31	36	26	7	100
Do something at home...					
with your partner	86	9	3	2	100
with your children	64	22	10	4	100
with friends	26	42	22	10	100
with another family member(s)	21	34	32	13	100
Go out and do something...					
with your partner	69	22	7	2	100
with your children	51	32	14	3	100
with friends	49	34	13	4	100
with another family member(s)	23	37	31	9	100
Sit down and talk one on one...					
with your partner	85	9	3	3	100
with your children	68	20	8	4	100
with a close friends	49	26	17	8	100
Engage in sex...	53	20	12	15	100
Attend a religious service...					
with your partner	21	8	25	46	100
with your children	14	8	26	52	100
with another family member(s)	7	8	33	52	100
Pray Privately...	51	11	11	27	100

Table 7.9. Some Personal Concerns by Age and Gender

% Indicating Concerned "A Great Deal" or "Quite A Bit"

	Nationally	Women	Men	18-34	35-54	55+
Never seem have enough time	53%	61	44	55	56	43
Lack of money	33	40	27	49	32	18
Your health	29	31	27	30	28	29
Loneliness	19	22	16	29	16	14
Boredom	11	14	8	17	10	6

As people across the country pursue health and happiness for themselves and their children, they obviously face more than relational strain. Poll after poll—including the current survey—invariably uncovers **three prominent immediate concerns of Canadians: time, money and health**. Then there are any number of additional issues that people have to deal with over the course of a lifetime.

The vast majority of Canadians (86%) describe their health as "excellent" or "good." Some 94% of those 18 to 34 make such a claim, compared to 87% of 35-to-54-year-olds, 78% of those between 55 and 74, and 70% who are 75 and older.

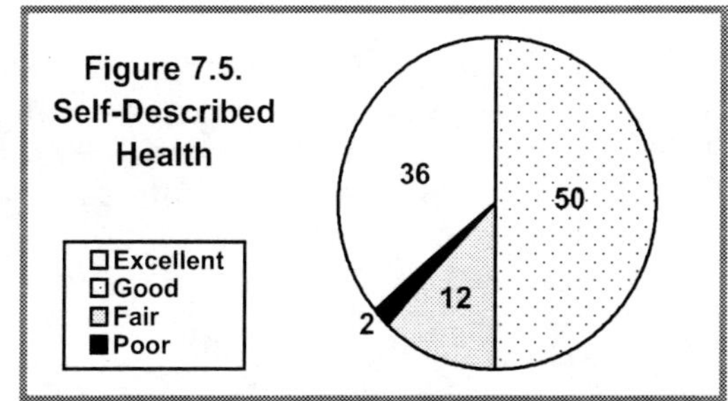

Figure 7.5. Self-Described Health

Given the prominent concern about lack of money, we asked Canadians, to complete the sentence, *"If I had more money, I would…."*

- Three priorities are each expressed by about 2 in 10 people: *family, travel and paying off bills.*
- More than 1 in 10 say they would share some of it with *other people*, including increasing what they give to charities.
- A further 1 in 10 say they would *retire early or quit their job.*
- Another 10% are divided between people who would *buy a house* and those who would *fix up their house.*
- The remainder (3%) say they would do things like spend the extra money on *friends*, plan for the f*uture and buy some things they want.*

Table 7.10. If I Had More Money

% Indicating Areas Where Would Spend It

Family	23%
Travel	21
Pay bills	19
Share it with others	14
Quit their jobs	10
Buy a house	6
Fix up my house	4
Friends	2
Other	1
Total	100

"If I Had More Money, I Would…."
Some Response Examples

...pay off my bills...travel more...save for my future...help my grandchildren...do something for myself...buy a new home and car...have kids...spend it... give more to those suffering hardship...see my children more...divide it with my grandkids...help others...buy luxurious things...take a break from my career...move...put away a nest egg...be very well off...continue as normal...go overseas...throw a huge party...indulge in more leisure...devote my life to singing...hire someone to paint the house...be able to be a stay at home with mom...pay off everyone's mortgages and travel with family...put it aside...support the church...buy real estate...retire early...move to Africa and work with an aid organization...pay back dad the money I borrowed for University...get out more...buy more clothes...stay home with my kids...get married...be truly happy...help children...have more freedom...get out from under debt...do exactly what I do now...visit home more often...hire a housekeeper...go back to school...move closer to work...worry less...make a down payment on a condo...give more to charity...start to enjoy my life more...help my children more...live better...look after my family more...be debt-free...buy Claudia Schiffer....we would work less and have more time together...retire...stop working and volunteer. ..buy an antique car...travel the world...draw, read and do things alone with my family...give more to my church...make my house bigger...have anything that I want...move to bigger centre...have more privacy...have my own business...do as I please...make sure all my friends and family were comfortable...go shopping...help people...upgrade my home and car...explore more activities...not be any happier...get in shape...establish personal security...ensure home-care for my Mom...create an education fund for my grandchildren...feel happier...pursue more of my personal interests...donate to the care of animals...go to the Mayo clinic...play more... volunteer more...have nicer things...buy a farm...take my son to Disneyland...quit my job...keep living my life the same way...pay off my student loan...go out with friends and partner more...live in Mexico...be more generous...I don't need more money...spend more time at home...not worry about money in my old age...buy more things...improve our standard of living...donate more to the community...help my parents out...perhaps change my present relationship...be done with school...buy a second Harley Davidson – everyone should have two...spend more time writing and recording songs and finance an album...be more at ease and enjoy life...take my wife on a trip...play more golf...live by myself...have a house on the lake...go into the office less...go out more in my wheelchair...splurge on my family...attend more cultural events....make sure my old age years will be taken care of...buy a house with a yard for my daughter...help less fortunate kids become good adults...have my wife at home full time...have a baby...move to Vancouver...leave the country...

We asked survey participants to complete another sentence relating to resources available to them in times of need. The item read, ***"When I face a serious problem, I turn to...."*** The question was open-ended and people typically offered two responses.

The number one resource they identify leads by a landslide—family.

- *Spouses and partners* are cited as key resources they turn to in times of need by close to 1 in 2 Canadians.

- *Family as a whole* is important for almost 1 in 5 people, and parents for almost 1 in 10.

- *Children and siblings* are each specifically cited as key resources by just 1 in 50 people.

- *Friends* are mentioned by 18%, only slightly ahead of the 15% who indicate that they find it helpful to turn to God and to prayer in times of need.

- Only 3 in 100 say that professional counsellors and caregivers are a primary resource for them in times of severe need, with less than 1 in 100 reporting that they turn to ministers, priests, and other religious figures.

Table 7.11.
Where Canadians Turn When Facing Serious Problems
More Than One Resource Could Be Cited

Family		73%
Spouse/partner	44	
Family generally	17	
Parents	8	
Children	2	
Siblings	2	
Friends		18
God & prayer		15
Myself		9
Professionals		3
General	3	
Clergy	<1	
No one		<1

As a final question, we asked Canadians, *"Is there ONE THING that would make your family life happier?"*

- Given that people's two primary personal concerns are money and time, it's not surprising that the most commonly cited "dreams" are having *more money* and having *more time*.

- Four other features are mentioned by fairly equal numbers of people: *a better relationship* with one's spouse or partner; *a society that is run better* by governments; *living closer* to one's family members; and having *better health*.

- The seventh wish cited by 3% of people is having a *better and safer world.*

It should be noted that 13% of people are content with things as they are in their lives.

Table 7.12
The Top Seven Things That Would Make Family Life Happier

1. Greater financial security	22%
2. Having more time	15
3. Imporved ties with my partner	6
4. A better-run society	6
5. Living closer to family	5
6. Better health	5
7. A better and safer world	3
* Content with things as they are	13

As for the lament about the need for a better-run society, it's clear that, for some people, frustrations about finances and time that, in turn, seriously impact individuals and families are linked to governments. As we saw earlier, next to family, Canadians see governments and schools as having the greatest responsibility for enhancing family life. They think life could be better.

What sometimes can be minimized in understanding why family life is not what it might be is the fact that large numbers of parents in particular are separated geographically from their children. Some 1 in 10 live in different provinces from the children; about 1 in 15 live in a different country.

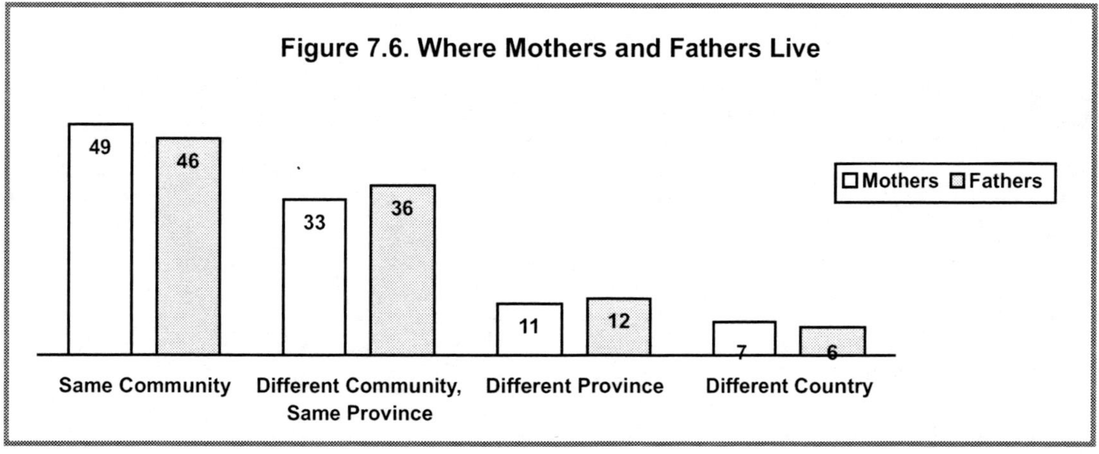

"Is there ONE THING that would make your family life happier?"
Some Response Examples

Finances
…no money problems…more money... being able to afford children...debts paid off...free post secondary education...some free child care, even one day a week...get a better paying job... better pay for teachers...additional funding for education...money and the time to spend it... less concern for material wealth... power to decide whether to work or stay home and not be penalized for it…my boys graduating from university debt-free…if mothers could stay home with their child until school age with 80% of their wages...more free activities instead of only ones that always cost money…more success in life...

Time
…having more quality time...being able to work less and sleep more...more time to do what I want to... more time together as a family…more time alone with my spouse...less frenetic activity in my life...more time with Daddy who works long hours so Mommy can stay home…a shorter work week…a change in society's expectations of having it all and working 24/7 to get it... if we could slow down our fast-paced life a little bit...more downtime, too many social pressures and expectations...some sleep…spending more time together…

A Better-Run Society
…honest government...intelligent government at all levels...resources that help parents understand change and development in children…support for stay at home mothers…get rid of the government…paying less taxes...a government that follows the bible...more government aid...lower cost of living…better tax breaks to encourage investing in one's future…government upholding marriage is man/woman…we are being taxed beyond measure…less government in our lives…

Living Closer
...seeing my grandchildren more...seeing my grandparents more...if my children in Vancouver lived in Montreal…being closer to friends...being geographically closer to family...

Health
…good health care…longer life expectancy...home care for the elderly...medical science finding cures for Parkinson's, Alzheimer's, etc...if my health was better...no cancer…that my husband's health would improve...my son's health...lead a healthier lifestyle...lose weight...having the government raise my disability payments…if my dad could walk more easily…

Companionship
…respect...less stress...acceptance...having someone to share family with...less conflict...mutual respect… more interaction…sharing a faith perspective...more love...having an emotionally stable partner that respected a strong, intelligent woman who is financially stable…me as a mother feeling less alone in my role...being accepted for who we are...

A Better and Safer World
...a more law-abiding society...stability in the world's situation...a perfect world...less violent society...a more peaceful world...a calmer world...an end to world problems...a more caring society…less crime and violence…

Relationships
...finding a partner...finding a wife...a girlfriend...having a companion...lose weight and find a partner...get married...a puppy...to be married...to meet someone special...a father figure for my child...be in a better relationship and have children...having kids...good men for my daughters…have a second child...have my own family…maybe some grandchildren…not having divorced parents…

Children
…more independent children...more activities for kids...accessible resources for dealing with the special needs of my child…knowing our son will be cared for in the event of our death…better relations with my sons...for my son to work...

Better Communication
…if my parents were more open to new ideas...kids that listen...if family members would listen to each other...sharing feelings and doing more things together...more family discussions about everything…

Other Thoughts
…not really...more involvement from relatives...being a closer family...less stress on young families...to care and share family values...to be able to get along with my mother…to be reunited with my family…having my deceased brother back...more sex...no, as a family we are doing fine... my whole family walking with God...travel more...a vacation…less alcohol...simplifying...decreasing the isolation from other families and communities....doing more things with my sons and daughter-in-law…if my partner hadn't died…teachers should be allowed to use more discipline...visitation enforcement…no, I'm extremely happy…

THE LONGER LOOK

Some Correlates of Placing High Value on the Family: 2000 and 1985

If "Highly" or "Moderately" Value Family Life...	***Importance Placed on the Family**** **2000** High	Moderate	**1985** High	Moderate
Very Highly Value...				
Friendship	82%	62	85	76
Forgiveness	74	48	79	53
Being a Canadian	61	40	72	45
Receive a High Level of Enjoyment from...				
The city or town one lives in	63	51	73	62
One's job	68	55	80	74
Have Group Involvement				
A member of an organization	68	67	77	73
Attend religious services at least once a month	31	22	41	19
Exhibit Social Compassion				
People who cannot afford it have a right to medical care	96	97	96	98
People who are poor have a right to an income adequate to live on	89	85	90	87

*Some 85% of Canadians in 2000 said family life is "very important" ('High') to them; another 13% indicated it is "somewhat important' ('Moderate'). Less than 2% said family life is "not important" to them.

Source: Reginald W. Bibby, Project Canada Survey Series.

Summary

When Canadians think of spending resources on families, their top priorities are health care and children. Everyone, they feel, should have access to good health care, regardless of age or income. As for children, people want to see them growing up in safe environments at home and school, free from exploitation and violence. In addition, respondents maintain that family priorities should include addressing the sustenance and employment needs of low-income parents. Significant numbers also maintain that attention should be given to helping individuals who are looking after elderly parents, strengthening marriages to reduce divorce, and providing financial support for parents—be they employed or raising their children at home.

In the minds of most people, the key sources to the well-being of children are parents who spend time with them, children feeling they are loved and children having good self-esteem. Canadians maintain that the primary tangible means of achieving such goals in addition to parents—are close friends, enjoyment of school, grandparents and siblings. Other sources, they say, are key individuals such as teachers and relatives, activities such as sports and, to a lesser extent, children's involvement in groups.

Asked where the responsibility lies for enhancing family life, almost all Canadians say it lies first and foremost with parents, followed by their offspring: for all its joy and pain, parenting is not viewed as a one-way street. Beyond family members, people say that schools and governments need to take a high level of responsibility for the enrichment of family life. Large numbers also say that other relatives, family agencies, religious groups, employers, the media and neighbourhoods also need to make contributions.

From a financial point of view, there is a widespread sense that governments need to take the lead in the case of post-secondary education, care for the elderly, and information and counselling for people requiring such services. Families, with some help from governments, should shoulder the primary financial responsibility for raising children, including child care and activities for young people. Communities, many say, should share costs with families and governments in providing both activities for youth, and information and counselling resources.

These survey findings underline why it is vitally important to enhance family life in Canada. The self-reports and hard data document the central role that families play in enriching the lives of Canadians. If we can find ways to deal with issues that impede family life and life more generally notably money, time, difficult relationships, and aging parents—family experiences can be better, and so can life for everyone involved.

Reflections: Canadians' Thoughts on Enhancing Family Life

The central importance that Canadians give to children is apparent when we learn from this survey that they give the same priority to children's well-being as they do to health care.

Canadians are also decisive in declaring that parents need to play the key role in enhancing the lives of their children and family life more generally. They maintain that it's essential for parents to spend time with their children, in the process making the primary contribution to children feeling both loved and valued. The contributions of other individuals and institutions are also called for, notably additional family members, friends and teachers. Adequate finances are also seen by many as important. But parents are paramount.

The survey also reveals that, in reality, large numbers of parents are having considerable difficulty realizing such expectations. Close to one in two employed parents, led by women—say they are troubled by the fact they are not spending enough time with their children. Close to the same number further admit that their children probably share the same view. The lack of time more generally is expressed by some 60% of women and 45% of men. In addition, lack of money is acknowledged as a source of anxiety for many, especially women and younger parents. And then there is the reality of divorce and separation: large numbers of parents are no longer together.

Two deductions seem obvious. The first is that, as a society, we need to find ways to provide parents with more financial security and make it possible for them to spend more time with their children. This is a particularly difficult challenge in the case of lone parents. But it also is a significant challenge for many two-parent families as well. Most people who are employed would be happy to work part-time, but say they have to work full-time to provide adequately for themselves and their children.

The good news is that there is evidence of a collective will to better support children and the parents who care for them. Although only about one in three Canadians maintain that child care support for parents who either are employed outside the home or choose to stay at home should be among our top priorities, almost an equal number are nonetheless in favour of governments (68%) sharing child-care costs with families (74%).

The second deduction is that children are among those who would benefit most if the incidence of divorce could be reduced. Close to 40% of Canadians maintain that strengthening marriage to prevent divorce should be given "very high" priority—almost double the number who think that such a priority should be given, for example, to helping families deal with the consequences of divorce. Moreover, as we

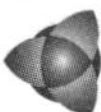

saw earlier, over 90% of Canadians favour "our society" helping people to have happy and lasting marriages by providing more counselling and information. Some 80% favour school courses on marriage and over 70% would like to see the media give marriage more support. In short, marriage needs to be strengthened by all our major institutions.

This last point is indicative of a more general finding that perhaps points to the prospect of stronger families in the future—the recognition on the part of Canadians that enhanced family life requires the efforts of everyone. It would be easy, for example, to point the finger of responsibility for less than optimum family life at government or schools or the media. However, the prevalent sentiment is that better family living will require the collective efforts of parents, children, institutions, and neighbourhoods, with the bills shared by governments, families, and communities.

Some Issues Raised by the Findings

1. Canadians' primary family priority is children. However, in the process of responding better to them, it is essential that older people not be neglected.

2. The balance between time needs and financial needs will probably never be perfect. But creative ways need to be explored to improve that balance so that life for families and their individual members can be enriched.

3. Families, along with friends, are Canadians' greatest sources of social capital. Greater effort needs to be made to recognize, support and tap the capacity of family members to care for one another and contribute to the well-being of their communities, which will, in turn, be better able to support their families.

What Does It All Mean

The Major Findings

There are at least four central findings that stand out from this survey.

The *first* is that the family continues to be of paramount importance to Canadians. It is experienced in a wide variety of ways. Nonetheless, the family is seen by almost everyone as an indispensable resource as people live out their lives.

The *second* is that the hopes and dreams of Canadians with respect to family life are, for the most part, fairly traditional.

The *third* is that the family realities which many people find themselves experiencing are anything but traditional.

The *fourth* is that some individuals choose to experience family life in ways that are not traditional.

1. The Importance of Family

The first point should not surprise anyone. After all, we all are "walking data." We need only to look at our own lives to realize the importance that partners, children, parents, siblings, grandparents, and any number of other relatives have had. Their value is underlined when they no longer are with us. Few obituaries are not centred around family members, followed, of course, by close friends. Family is simply at the heart of our lives.

2. The Hopes and Dreams Are Fairly Traditional

The second point initially troubles some: what people would like to experience in the way of family life tends to be fairly traditional. To make such a statement is to sound like a right wing traditional family advocate, harking back to days of yore and a world that no longer exists and perhaps never really existed beyond our imaginations. But hear me out: what I mean is that the vast majority of Canadians aspire to marry, to have children who are happy and healthy, to be good parents, to have lasting relationships, to care for aging parents, and in their later years if necessary be cared for themselves. That's what most people want. Let no critic of the traditional family ideal get away with claims that such aspirations no longer exist. The traditional family ideal remains pervasive in Canada in these early years of the new century.[40]

3. The Family Realities Are Often Far From Traditional

But, for most people, the traditional family is just that—an ideal. No, it's not that the majority of people don't want most of those things that are linked to the traditional family. If we need a quick reminder of traditional aspirations, we only have to listen to teenagers who, regardless of their own home experiences, are telling us— 90% strong— that they plan to marry, have children, and stay with the same partner for the rest of their lives. It's just that as life unfolds, things don't always work out the way everyone planned. Life is dynamic. People change, people disappear, circumstances change. Along the way, what seemed readily attainable becomes highly elusive. It's not necessarily anyone's fault. It's just the way life is.

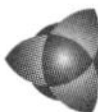

You can think of illustrations just as readily as I can.

- My friend Lee who was in her mid-20s, married to Dave, the person of her dreams, and pregnant with their first child. The condominium was being built and was paid for. Everything seemed perfect. And then one stormy morning, Dave was killed in a single plane crash. That's how some single mothers come into being.

- My own mother had vibrant young parents in their early thirties who had come to Canada from rural Wales. One day, with no warning, her father died of mushroom poisoning, leaving a single mother with four little children. A few years later, her mother remarried an older family friend. That's how some stepparents come into being.

- Every one of us can think of a married couple that seemed to have it all, yet a few years were alienated and demoralized. That's how some divorces come into being—that lead to the emergence of single parents who in turn remarry and contribute to any number of new family configurations.

- And who would have thought that a person who seemed as loving and responsible as he was would one day become the alcoholic father who would beat his wife and make his young children afraid to come home.

People do not always get what they want.

4. Not everyone opts for what is traditional.
To the extent that Canadians have a choice in the matter, some, of course, do not have traditional or conventional aspirations. They include those who consciously decide not to marry or not to have children. Some want children but do not want marriage or even a relationship. A sizeable or non-trivial number choose to establish same-sex relationships. A relatively small number may wish to distance themselves from family members in favour of friends.

Table 8.1. The Growing Diversity of Families in Canada: 1931 -2001

	1931	**1951**	**1971**	**1991**	**2001**
Married couples with children at home	55%	58	60	48	42
Married couples without children at home	31	32	31	29	29
Common-law couples with children at home	**	**	**	4	6
Common-law couples without children at home	**	**	**	6	7
Lone-parents	14	10	9	13	16

Source: Adapted from Statistics Canada, Census Family Time Series.

The Major Responses

In a society such as ours that aspires to be both pluralistic and compassionate in elevating life for all people, each of these four key findings about family life carries with it some basic but important implications for responses. To varying degrees, of course, we are currently responding in the ways I am delineating. Insofar as we are, these thoughts serve as a reminder of what we need to keep doing. In some instances, however, it also is clear that we need to do better.

1. The Importance of Family

Our public debates about the quality of life in Canada invariably focus on issues that are seen as affecting individuals. One thinks of the attention given health, the economy, crime, poverty, abuse, and so on. In light of the importance that the family has in the lives of individuals, it seems to me that there is a great need for politicians, policy-makers, and other key decision-makers to reframe many public issues in family as well as individual terms. How do health care and economic issues affect families? If crime makes people feel unsafe in their communities and violence makes people feel unsafe in their homes, what is the impact on family life?

In short, the unit of analysis we typically use in attempting to enhance our quality of life is the individual. That obviously is very important. But the unit of analysis that requires at least equal attention in the enrichment of both individual and social life is family.

2. The Hopes and Dreams Are Fairly Traditional

To the extent that Canadians aspire to have traditional kinds of family life, we need to respond, not with derision and cynicism, but by doing everything we can to help them to better understand and realize their aspirations. One would assume that one reason that such widespread hopes and dreams have emerged is because people believe that the best features of traditional family life work reasonably well. Individuals need to better understand what is involved in pursuing such related ideals, in relationship to other values such as freedom, independence and career success. The fact that many people have not been able to realize their dreams should not be confused with people necessarily being happy with either where they are or how they got there, or being applauded for contributing to family diversity. Despite how things may look, traditional family dreams persist for most people.

3. The Family Realities Are Often Far From Traditional

Insofar as large numbers of people, for very diverse reasons, have not been able to realize some of their family dreams, we as a society need to do all we can to help them to optimize their family situations, whatever they may be. As we have seen, there are many financial and emotional costs associated with such developments as marriages breaking down, partners dying young, people trying to combine careers with parenting, individuals attempting to remarry and blend families, and grandparents trying to cope with it all. Lots of people are in need of help.

4. Not Everyone Opts for What is Traditional

To the extent that people have choices about what kind of family life they will have—and most of us do, at least as younger people—it is essential that they are provided with the opportunity to reflect on the options available, so that they can make informed choices that serve them and our society best.

Our Canadian emphasis on diversity should not lead us to naively assume that everything leads to the same result.[40] We need to continue to study and encourage reflection on the outcomes of various family choices. All of our major institutions must provide opportunities for diverse voices to be heard so that good decisions can be made.

Getting Specific

This brings me back to the primary findings of the survey and to some of the issues that I have raised at the end of each of the seven sections of the report.

1. The Nature of Family
A majority of Canadians indicate that they hold the traditional family as ideal, with even a greater majority saying that it is their personal choice. We need to reflect on why this is the case, taking into consideration the desire of most people both to marry and have children. In short, functionally-speaking, how does the traditional family "work," compared to other structural possibilities? When is it functional and when might it be dysfunctional?

Obviously we are all free to choose whatever arrangement we want. But we need to understand the benefits and costs of the options we choose. If, having examined the balance sheet, conventional family arrangements are what most people want, and the personal and social benefits are evident, we need to help people to experience them.

Beyond the traditional family, in light of the premier importance that Canadians place on family life generally, everything possible needs to continue to be done to elevate family life in all its varied forms. People across the country are convinced that families are essential to both personal and social well-being, contributing to healthy communities and a healthy nation. Leaders who claim to care about Canadians and Canadian life are therefore left with a very strong mandate to give the enhancement of families extremely high priority.

2. Dating, Sexuality and Cohabitation
Sexual behaviour prior to marriage is often a source of disagreement among Canadians. Some parents tell us that only abstinence is appropriate for adolescents, while others support birth control for teenagers. However, below the surface of fairly superficial survey readings on the extent to which people "approve" of such conduct, Canadians remain strongly divided when it comes to actual approval, versus what amounts to tolerance. We would benefit from having more open discussions that help us understand more clearly the distinction between approval and acceptance, the bases for such positions, and the implications for the people involved.

Homosexuality is also a topic that continues to be widely discussed. The strong division of opinion documented by the survey points to the need for ongoing reflections that similarly help us to understand the reasoning behind the levels of approval, acceptance and rejection. This is an area in which rhetoric and name-calling are common, indicative of the division that frequently exists in place of respect for diversity. We have to do better at reducing the hostility - associated with such polarized views.[42]

The increasing incidence of ***cohabitation*** outside of marriage is clearly something that carries its pluses and minuses. The preliminary examination of some of the survey results indicates that, on balance, people living common-law are experiencing more strain and lower levels of enjoyment than those who are married. These findings are consistent with some recent studies.[43] However, we need a much better understanding of the relative merits of marriage versus cohabitation. More formal research, discussions and reflections are required.

3. Marriage
The survey has found that the overwhelming majority of Canadian adults have either been married or plan to marry. In addition, marriage is on the drawing board for some nine in ten teenagers. Still further, almost everyone who has been married, is married or plans to marry aspires to stay with the same partner for life.

If that's the case, it pretty much goes without saying that a responsible society will ensure that people are prepared for marriage, so that they can be both good and lasting. This isn't merely the job of a minister who puts couples through a quick marriage prep course. It's the job of all our major institutions. We have to find more effective ways to support marriage, while at the same time encouraging encourage Canadians to be critically informed about the nature of marriage and the expectations that accompany it.

The survey documents the fact that sizeable numbers of young Canadians are not giving up on marriage so much as postponing it. This is part of a series of delays identified by University of Western Ontario sociologist Roderic Beaujot in his report released earlier this year entitled, *Delayed Life Transitions: Trends and Implications*. According to Beaujot, over the past four decades, all the major transitions of the younger years have been occurring later—when people finish school, start to work full-time, leave home, marry, and have children. The trend has important implications for other age groups and, of course, for fertility. He maintains that greater societal investments are needed in areas including post-secondary education, the school to work transition, and the having and raising of children.[44] Such investments presumably would also serve to facilitate and strengthen marriage.

As with support for traditional family aspirations, support for marriage should not and does not have to be at the expense of being disparaging toward people who do not choose to marry. Efforts to better understand why so many Canadians want to marry obviously need to include the opportunity both to understand and appreciate why some individuals prefer other options.

4. Children, Hopes and Values

Our society seems well attuned to the ***central importance*** that people place on children. The survey findings confirm that such a priority needs to be maintained and, if anything, given more of our institutional time and resources.

Canadians feel strongly about the importance of adults being reflective about ***having children***. They feel prospective parents need to recognize the responsibilities involved in being parents, being prepared—for example—to give children considerable time. In light of the value most place on having two parents present, 95% of Canadians also feel that it is important for people considering parenthood to have strong relationships with their partners. These kinds of values associated with responsible parenthood, along with why they are held, require considerable discussion and reflection. In light of their pervasiveness and apparent merit, they also warrant societal-wide support.

For all the rhetoric about the relativity and personal nature of ***values***, the survey shows a very high level of consensus concerning the importance of instilling in children traits that include honesty, personal responsibility, getting along with others, politeness, reliability, and concern for others. Despite the general importance we place on civility, it is not at all clear that these kinds of values that contribute to it are receiving widespread and explicit institutional support. If Canadians are correct in asserting that instilling such values is important to the enhancement of individual and social life, the situation has to change. We need to create environments where people of all ages can reflect on the nature and significance of interpersonal values, and consciously and intentionally encourage the adoption of those values.

5. Parenting and Parents

Virtually all Canadians agree that ***parents should take equal responsibility*** for raising children and for carrying out household duties. The ongoing problem documented by our survey is the fact that many males are not coming through, and in the process are putting extra weight on the shoulders of their female partners.[45] Mothers who are employed outside the home are feeling particularly strained. Their numbers are significant: the 60% of women who are currently in the labour force (versus about 30% in 1961) include about 65% of mothers with children under six and 60% with children under the age of two.[46] Many observers for some time now have drawn attention to the issue. It's no laughing matter: many mothers continue to be stressed out. It's time for us to give the problem high priority, by way of improving life for women, children and our society as a whole.

It needs to be noted that, even when employed mothers do indicate that their partners are "coming through," it still is not always possible for women to balance careers and parenting to their own satisfaction. In some cases part-time employment might be a solution—but not usually for those who are beginning highly competitive careers. Nor is quitting necessarily a perfect solution, given the negatives relating to income, career advancement and self-esteem. In a recent interview, the CBC's Wendy Mesley, the mother of a five-year-old daughter, expressed things this way: "Working is part of what makes me 'me'. I can't imagine staying home full-time. I would love to have a half-job, but all the really good jobs in journalism require a fair commitment." [47]

Table 8.2. The Employed Labour Force: 1981 and 2001

Full-time (30+ Hours Weekly) and Part-time (<30 Hours) Work

	1981	**2001**
NATIONALLY		
Full-time	85%	82%
Part-time	15	18
Average hours per week	*39*	*39*
Men: ***% of Employed Labour Force***	**60**	**54**
Full-time	92	88
Part-time	8	12
Average hours per week	*42*	*42*
Women: ***% of Employed Labour Force***	**40**	**46**
Full-time	74	74
Part-time	26	26
Average hours per week	*34*	*35*

Source: Computed from Statistics Canada, 1981 Census and 2001 Census, Catalogue no. 97F0012XCB01005.

A heavy weight, is, of course, falling on people—usually women but sometimes men—who do not even have the luxury of a partner who potentially can help with parenting tasks. In addition to governments, such people would benefit, and in some instances, are benefiting from the assistance of community resources, starting with friends, neighbours and organizations that in some cases include churches and other religious groups. More such help appears to be required.

Many parents who are employed outside the home indicate that they are in need of some ***child care*** help. In a perfect world, people say that if they had a choice, the caregiver would be one of the parents. That would please most Canadians, since 90% agree that, when the children are preschoolers, it would be preferable for one of the parents to stay home. The familiar problem here, of course, is that work schedules often do not make such an arrangement possible. Also, in a good number of instances, the head of the family is a single parent. The additional options posed by most people are for grandparents to become involved, followed in preference by other family members. If those possibilities are not viable, the next choice is a child care setting.

These findings suggest that, to the extent that governments become financially involved, they are being asked to give serious thought to doing more than providing funding for formal child care possibilities. Canadians favour policies that will result in funds being directed toward the primary child care choices of parents —*first*, mothers and fathers who would prefer to stay home—in some instances working part-time, *second* grandparents or other relatives, and *third*, formal child care settings. However, if, as some academics claim, quality child care has the potential to contribute more to children's well-being than parents seem to realize, a better job needs to be done of showing them why this is the case. The Quebec experience obviously bears watching. In recent years, that province has opted to move from a tax deduction for child-care of all kinds to providing low cost, professionally run child-care.[48]

The survey has also documented the extensive care needs of ***aging Canadians***. But it also has uncovered the encouraging finding that around 90% of people across the country have indicated that they would be willing to look after their parents "if they needed me to do so." Of the some 40% of seniors who are not living in their own homes or apartments, less than 10% are currently living with their children. Government policies aimed at addressing the needs for care among older Canadians obviously should be highly cognizant of the willingness of significant numbers of sons (91%) and daughters (86%) to play a greater role in that care of their parents. As with child care, there is reason to believe that, at least in a good number of instances, resources might best be spent supplementing home environments rather than replacing them.

6. When Relationships End
Survey respondents who have gone through a divorce or separation were hardly glib in telling about their experiences. Most, especially women, were adamant about the fact that the termination of their relationships ***was absolutely necessary***. Most also acknowledged that the break up was hard on them emotionally; those with children say it was difficult for them as well. A majority further indicated that it created financial problems for them. The ripple effect did not stop at home: some one in two people who experienced divorce or separation reported that it had been hard on their parents. The same proportion said it affected their performance at work. Large numbers of children corroborated the negative impact of divorce on their lives.

In short, divorce—despite its acknowledged necessity—is something that has ***carried a big price tag*** for large numbers of individuals, as well as many of their social environments. In light of its personal and social costs, there would seem to be considerable value in our re-examining the extent to which divorce is necessary.

If the costs are so great, we as a society—as with anything that has a negative impact on our quality of life—would be advised to find better ways to help people ***avoid divorce***, while ensuring that it remains an option for people who absolutely need it. Our respondents are not lost for some basic ideas. Strong majorities would like to see more counselling and more information to help people with their marriages. Eight in ten would like to see courses on marriage in our schools; seven in ten say marriage should receive more support from the media. Significantly, there is far more support for giving "very high" priority to being proactive rather than reactive—strengthening marriages rather than dealing with the consequences of divorce.

Such efforts to reduce divorce, however, must not have the regressive side effect of having a negative impact on people who experience it. Far fewer younger adults whose parents divorced indicate that they experienced stigma compared to their older counterparts. As a society we have to ensure that the trend away from negative labelling and disadvantage continues.

7. Responding to Family Hopes and Dreams
The survey findings on the priorities that Canadians feel we should be giving to a variety of family issues call us to reflect on ***what people want versus what seems to be taking place***. On the surface, there appears to be reasonably good matches between expectations and the high priority that governments are giving to health care, a number of child-related matters, and assistance of various kinds to low-income parents. It is not as clear that governments and other institutions are giving the "very high priority" rating requested by almost one in two Canadians to providing help for those who are caring for elderly parents, or such a premier priority hoped for by one in three respondents to strengthening marriages or providing child care support. Are these disparities that warrant being rectified?

One of the most difficult challenges facing parents is how to find a good balance between ***having enough time and having enough money***. The time issue is particularly important: Canadians believe that what is indispensable to healthy and happy children are parents who spend time with them. Few are speaking theoretically; most are speaking from personal experience.

To the extent we take such concerns seriously, as a society, we need to reflect on the extent to which the resolution of the time-money issue lies with individuals, versus with our institutions, notably governments. Should we be putting the primary onus on governments to provide parents with more money in order to free up more time? Should parents be encouraged, for example, to alter their career aspirations—or as no one seems to dare to mention—where possible, consider modifying their consumption expectations in favour of spending more time at home with their children? Are there other players—such as employers and the business sector, community organizations and religious groups—with significant roles to play? Resolutions obviously are difficult to find. But they need to be aggressively pursued.

Canadians are not passing the buck when it comes to their views on ***who's responsible*** for enhancing family life, or who should be paying the bills. They are reasonable in recognizing that they as parents and children and other family members have key roles to play, and further readily acknowledge the supportive presence of friends. But they also recognize that they require the help of their governments and their communities, and, in many instances, their schools, family agencies, and religious groups.

It all adds up to a situation where Canadians supremely value family life. For most individuals, families are both their greatest source of enjoyment and their key resource for living. Strong families require the support of the rest of Canadian society. Significantly, the support is not one-way: in turn, they have much to give.

Conclusion

In initiating this project, we did so with one primary goal in mind: we wanted to get a clear reading on what Canadians want from family life. We recognized that there is much adaptation evident in the family lives of people these days. We are aware that the realities of people's lives often depart from their own ideals and aspirations. Further, there is a varied range of societal responses to how Canadians have tried to make sense out of the lives they have consciously fashioned for themselves or have experienced because of the circumstances they have encountered. There also has been a considerable amount of research that has sought to monitor what's been taking place. In the midst of all this adaptation and monitoring, we felt there was value in asking people to "take a quick breather" from their family realities and tell us what, in fact, they want from family life. In keeping with such a goal, the questionnaire carried the title, *The Future Families Project*, with the subtitle, *A Survey of Canadian Hopes and Dreams*.

Confronted by the data that point to a larger proportion of common-law relationships and a corresponding decrease in the number and proportion of marital relationships, many journalists and academics are inclined to claim that the family as we have known it going the route of the dinosaur. For example, on the heels of the October 2002 release of the latest census findings on the family, Tom Arnold of *The National Post* wrote, "The institution known as Canada's traditional family—a married mother and father with children—is crumbling." [49] Similarly, Canadian Press, in a widely distributed story, declared, "'Traditional' no longer describes the universal ideal for family in Canada. Modern Canadians are not content to simply find a mate, hit the altar and live happily ever after." [50] The *Globe and Mail*'s Erin Anderssen succinctly summed up things this way: "Canada is a place of loners and shrinking families, where the lovers have increasingly lost interest in a walk down the aisle." [51] Two recent articles in *Maclean's* have asserted that increasing numbers of women are no longer waiting for men before having children on their own, and that, for many adults, friends have taken the place of family.[52] A decade ago in 1994, the United Nation's International Year of the Family, a major national poll conducted for the magazine led to the conclusion that "the 1950s-style family, though not quite extinct, is on the endangered list." Still, the poll pointed to the family showing "enduring strength." [53]

That enduring strength is readily apparent in our survey results. Contrary to much of what is being written and said, we have found considerable consensus in the way Canadians conceptualize families, as well as in what they want from family life. Sociologist Robert Brym has been among those who have cautioned about prematurely assuming the demise of the family. In his words, the available evidence "should not lead one to conclude that the family is in a state of collapse. The overwhelming majority of adults still want to marry and have children." Brym adds, "The family is not a crumbling institution. What is happening, however, is that people are freer than they once were to establish the kinds of family arrangements that best suit them." [54]

During my initial visit to the Vanier Institute in Ottawa in December of 2002, I came across a framed declaration that is mounted on a hallway wall. It was written by Prime Minister Lester B. Pearson in 1967. He commends to all Canadians the plans and purposes of a new institute for the family, and asks for their support, describing it as a new and significant Canadian undertaking.

The Prime Minister wrote that he was proud to say that the Canadian government was making a sizeable contribution toward the establishment of the endowment fund required to support the Institute. That support was based on three considerations: the Government's deep respect for the lifetime service of the Governor-General and Madame Vanier, an endorsement of the Institute as a Centennial project worthy of the widest possible Canadian support, and "the Government's concern that the aims of the Institute be realized—the strengthening of family life in Canada as a basis on which our nation's moral strength and vitality depend." He added,

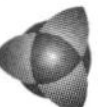

The Canadian concern for the well-being of family life in our country knows no provincial boundary. It is shared as well by all our different faiths and communions, and they—like the Government of Canada—look to the Vanier Institute of the Family to become a vital force in the welfare of Canadian family life.

Some four decades later, the findings of this survey support the late Prime Minister's assertions about the pervasive importance that Canadians place on the well-being of families. The findings also document the fact that, in the midst of claims of growing family diversity and the relativity of the personal and social outcomes associated with that diversity, some things perhaps have not changed as much as we thought. Canadians continue to have much in common when it comes to their family aspirations. For better or worse, most envision marrying and staying with the same partner; having children who are happy and healthy, responsible and caring; looking after their parents as necessary; and enjoying their children and grandchildren. They recognize that they need others to bring it all off. But most want to believe such dreams are within their grasp.

Unfortunately, as their lives unfold, many Canadians older and younger find that what they hoped for is not what is taking place. They continue on, often remarrying, trying to adjust to additional children and siblings and new fathers, new mothers, and new in-laws—while parents and grandparents attempt to keep up with it all.

Then there are others who opt for less traditional family forms but, like everyone else, sometimes find that things do not work out as well as they hoped. Money and time are often short, commitment is not always lasting, stigma is frequently encountered.

In the midst of all the diversity, Canadians cherish family life and want it to work. Why? Because they need it. And society needs it.

It's my hope that the family aspirations and dreams expressed to us by people from coast to coast will be given the hearing and responses that they deserve. If the Prime Minister was right in 1967, what's at stake is not only the happiness and well-being of individuals and families, but also the enhanced health and vitality of the nation.

NOTES

Section 1 The Nature of Family

[1] Statistics Canada, for purposes of the 2000 census, emphasized the presence of couples and/or children in defining the family as "*a married couple (with or without children of either or both spouses), a couple (with or without children of either or both partners), or a lone parent of any marital status, with at least one child living in the same dwelling.*" It added that a couple living common-law may be either opposite or same sex, and that "children" in a census family may include grandchildren living with their grandparent(s) with no parents present. The definition provided by the Vanier Institute of the Family is frequently drawn upon in reflections on family life. According to its official definition, couples and children may or may not be present: "*...any combination of two or more persons who are bound together over time by ties of mutual consent, birth and/or adoption or placement and who, together, assume responsibilities for variant combinations of some of the following...*". The Institute proceeds to list, as areas of potential responsibility, physical maintenance of group members, addition of new members, socialization of children, social control of members, production, consumption, distribution of goods and services, and affective nuturance (love). See the VIF website www.vifamily.ca. One well-respected family sociologist, Bonnie Fox of the University of Toronto, offers the following definition in Canada's most widely used introductory sociology text: "*..I define* family *as the sets of relationships people create to share resources daily in order to ensure their own and any dependants' welfare.*" We obviously were well aware of the complexity involved in using the term "family" as we began work on this project. That's why, from a methodological point of view, rather than imposing definitions on Canadians, we started our survey conversation by asking them what *they* have in mind when they speak of families.

[2] For the purposes of this report, the traditional or conventional family refers to a married man and woman with one or more children. Also referred to as the "nuclear family".

[3] As noted in the "Background" section of the report, comparisons with census data for 2001 suggest our respondents mirror the marital status characteristics of the population fairly well.

[4] Various Statistics Canada publications report that the birth rate (births per 1000 population) in Canada stood at 23.2 in 1931 and 26.1 in 1961; however, it fell to 15.7 by 1976 and to an all-time low of 10.5 in 2002. The fertility rate (estimate of the average number of children women 15 to 49 will have in their lifetime) was 1.5 in 2002, compared to 1.8 in 1976 and 3.4 in 1931. The 2001 census found the average household size was 2.6 people, down from 2.9 in 1981 (Statistics Canada, *The Daily*, October 22, 2002).

[5] The trend toward older offspring remaining at home longer was also documented in the 2001 census, where 41% of young adults under 30 were living with their parents (Statistics Canada, catalogue no. 96F0030XIE2001003).

[6] The 2001 census found that some 13% *of parents* were living with their children at the time the census was taken (Statistics Canada, catalogue no. 96F0030XIE2001003). Our figure of 4% refers to the percentage *of adults* who have a parent or grandparent who has resided with them for more than one year. The figures are complementary, but probe two different questions.

[7] One recent study, Statistics Canada's Participation and Activity Limitation Survey (PALS) conducted in 2001, found that 4% of children between the ages of 5 and 14 and 14% of adults had some form of "activity limitation" (see *The Daily*, March 25, 2003 and July 29, 2003). Our survey has found that some 2% of Canadian adults under the age of 35 indicate they have a major disability.

Section 2 Dating, Sexuality and Cohabitation

[8] The 2001 census found that, among Canadians 15 and older, 8% were in common-law relationships, with the figure for Quebec 17%. Our 2003 survey figures of 12% and 22% respectively do not appear to be out of line, given our sample is comprised of Canadians 18 and over, and that there probably has been a slight increase in such relationships since 2001 (Statistics Canada, catalogue no. 95F0487XCB01001).

[9] In its release of 2001 census findings on the family entitled, *Profile of Canadian Families and Households* (catalogue no. 96F0030XIE2001003), Statistics Canada noted that although a growing number of young adults are likely to "start their conjugal life through a common-law relationship," some 75% can be expected to marry if current trends continue.

[10] A Statistics Canada release, summarizing some key findings on common-law relationships from the 2001 General Social Survey, expressed things this way: "Common-law relationships have different meanings for different generations. Among the young, it is a prelude to, or substitute for, a first marriage; among older people, common-law unions are generally a prelude to, or substitute for, remarriage" (*The Daily*, July 11, 2002).

[11] « Ecclesiastes I, 9 »

Section 3 - Marriage

[12] In 1975, the first marriage average age of brides was 22.0, grooms 24.4; as of 2001, the averages were 28.2 and 30.1 respectively (Statistics Canada and *The Daily*, November 20, 2003).

[13] A Statistics Canada General Social Survey in 2001 found that 82% of adults had been married by religious clergy in the case of first marriages, with the figure slipping to 66% for remarriages (*The Daily*, November 20, 2003).

[14] These figures are consistent with the Statistics Canada figures for first marriages since 1975 noted above.

[15] See Bibby, *Canada's Teens*, Toronto: Stoddart/Novalis, 2001:135,199-200.

[16] A January 2004 Ipsos Reid poll found that a very similar 47% of Canadians approved of same sex marriages.

[17] In 2002, for example, one-quarter of all violent crimes reported to a sample of Canadian police services involved cases of family violence. Rates currently stand at about 345 per 100,000 for women and 60 per 100,000 for men (Statistics Canada, *Family Violence in Canada: A Statistical Profile*, 2003 and 2004). Victimization reports obviously point to a much higher level of violence than that reported to the police. The 1999 GSS survey, for example, found that 8% of women and 7% of men in relationships had experienced some kind of violence over the previous five-year period (*The Daily*, July 25, 2000).

[18] Recent condemnation of provincial funding for a school at a polygamous commune in British Columbia illustrates the strong, ongoing opposition to the possibility of multiple marriage partners (see Canadian Press article on the Bountiful school in Lister, BC, July 2, 2003).

[19] The 2001 GSS examination of common-law marriages concluded that individuals who cohabit or have lived common-law and then marry are considerably more likely to divorce than those who started their conjugal relationships with marriage, even in Quebec (*The Daily*, July 11, 2002).

Section 4 Children, Hopes and Values

[20] What this difference reflects in large part is the growing inclination for parents to have children later. In 1982, mothers in their 20s gave birth to 66% of babies; by 2002 the figure had dropped to 48%. Mothers in their 30s gave birth to 23% of all babies in 1982, compared to 45% in 2002 (*The Daily*, April 19, 2004).

[21] As noted earlier, these averages are consistent with the declining fertility rate 3.4 in 1931, 1.8 in 1976, and 1.5 in 2002. Obviously the current average of about 2.4 children reflects different fertility rates over time.

[22] As many readers are well aware, social and support groups have been established for individuals and couples who do not have children. One of the better known is *No Kidding*, an organization with worldwide chapters that was founded in Vancouver in 1986 "for adult couples and singles who, for whatever reason, have never had children," and declares, "We are a social club nothing more, nothing less." For further information, see www.nokidding.net.

[23] Statistics Canada reports that the average age of first-time mothers in 2002 was 27.7 (*The Daily*, April 19, 2004).

Section 5 Parenting and Parents

[24] According to the 2001 census, 66% of women under the age of 25 with marital or common-law partners were employed, as were 75% of those in such relationships who were between the ages of 25 and 44. Those under 25 with no children had an employment rate of 79%, compared to 51% for those with one child, 40% for those with two, and 30% for those with three children (2001 Census, Statistics Canada, catalogue no, 95F0379XCB01003).

[25] Respected Sociologist Bonnie Fox is among those who argue that both mothers and children benefit from a balance between home and outside employment, homecare and outside child care: "A single, isolated caregiver inevitably loses some inspiration, enthusiasm, and even warmth over the course of 24 hours a day, seven days a week. Moreover, the home is not designed for toddlers; it is both dangerous and less stimulating than it should be" (Fox in Robert Brym, ed. *New Society*, 4th edition. Toronto: Thomson-Nelson, 2004:322).

[26] Statistics Canada's GSS Survey has consistently identified the same finding. In 1998, for example, time stress levels were highest for married women and men between 25 and 44 who were employed full-time with children at home. Some 38% of women and 26% of men in this group reported they were time-stressed (*The Daily*, November 9, 1999). Similar findings are offered by the National Population Health Survey spanning 1994 to 2001 (*The Daily*, January 21, 2004).

[27] A June 2001 poll by Leger and Leger, reported by Canadian Press, found that 53% of Canadians believed gays and lesbians should be able to adopt children.

[28] The first Statistics Canada survey to ask about sexual orientation was carried out in 2003. The Canadian Community Health Survey of 135,000 people, 12 and over, found that 1% considered themselves to be homosexual and an additional .7% bisexual. The figures for men were 1.3% and 6% respectively; for women, .7% and .9%. They based those figures on survey participants 18 to 59 (*The Daily*, June 15, 2004). Our survey has found a slightly higher, 2.3% of respondents to indicate they are gay or lesbian, with another .5 reporting they are bisexual. We have combined the homosexual and bisexual figures in Figure 5.4. The fact that our survey was conducted by mail and theirs partly by telephone by a government agency, and with people 60 and over excluded may account for the slight difference in results.

[29] Given such public attitudes, it is not surprising that federal legislation was prepared in late 2003 that would prohibit the creation of a human clone.

[30] Census data on the living arrangements of older Canadians, organized in somewhat different ways from what appears in this report, can be found in the *Profile of Canadian Families and Households* (catalogue no. 96F0030XIE2001003).

[31] One reason some express strain is suggested by some 2001 census findings. An analysis has found that 1% of all grandparents were living with their grandchildren, without either of the child's parents involved. Just under one-half of the children were under the age of 15. In 65% of these shared households, grandparents carried the financial responsibility ("Across the Generations: Grandparents and Grandchildren," *Canadian Social Trends*, Winter, 2003).

Section 6 When Relationships End

[32] Statistics Canada reports that 60% of divorces in 2002 involved people married for less than 15 years. The divorce rate peaked at about 2 per 1,000 in the fourth year after marriage, decreasing steadily for every year after that. The average duration of marriage for those divorcing was 14 years (*The Daily*, May 4, 2004).

[33] Many observers have maintained that financial strain is one of the central consequences of divorce, particularly for women and children. In 2002, for example, the pre-tax median total income of couple families was $61,200, compared to $28,100 for lone-parent families (*The Daily*, May 26, 2004).

[34] In 2001, the average age of previously married brides was 41.4, grooms 45.0. The average age of previously widowed brides was 56.4, previously widowed grooms 62.9 (*The Daily*, November 20, 2003).

Section 7 Responding to Family Hopes and Dreams

[35] The GSS for 2001 found that 5 in 10 stepfamilies contained only the mother's children and just 1 in 10 only the father's offspring. The remaining 4 in 10 were "blended." In 81% of these latter cases, the new couple had a child or children in addition to a child or children they brought into the relationship (*The Daily*, July 11, 2002).

[36] While it will surprise few people in social agencies, companies, and the media that Canadians are looking to them to enhance family life, much-maligned religious leaders need to take seriously the mandate they are receiving from some four in ten Canadians.

[37] A 2003 Statistics Canada report, *Part-Time Work and Family-Friendly Practices in Canadian Workplaces (71-584-MIE)*, found that most companies do not foster climates that promote the integration of work and family. Some 1 in 3 employees did report having flextime options, but these were frequently limited to smaller companies with fewer than 10 employees. In addition, women had lower participation rates in flexible work arrangements than men. The role of employers in enriching social life is also highlighted in a recent article in the Statistics Canada publication, *Perspectives on Labour and Income*. Close to 50% of employed volunteers received employer support in the form of time-off or the changing of hours. See *The Daily*, April 22, 2003.

[38] The 2003 General Social Survey focused on Social Engagement. It also documents the central importance of family and friends and the relative importance of community (see 2003 GSS, "An Overview of Findings," 89-598-XIE).

[39] The initial overview of findings for the 2003 GSS on Social Engagement unfortunately disregards its own data in downplaying the importance to Canadians of religious groups. There is no single organization to which more people belong or in which they are involved on an active or semi-active basis. See the overview listed above, as well as my own recent book, *Restless Churches* (Wood Lake/Novalis, 2004), which also gives some clarity to "the God footnote."

Section 8 What Does It All Mean

[40] Some observers write as if current preferred family forms are essentially "up for grabs." American sociologist Judith Stacey, for example, has written, "No longer is there a single culturally dominant family pattern." She maintains that the postmodern family stands for a variety of contemporary family cultures such as families of colour, single parent families, same-sex couples, and extended families (Stacey, "The Post-Modern Family." In Charles Lemert (ed.). *Social Theory: The Multicultural and Classic Readings*. Boulder, CO: Westview Press, 1999:647).

[41] As a number of observers notably Robert Bellah and Alan Bloom have reminded us in recent years, there are some serious limitations to blindly heralding the virtues of diversity and relativism (Bloom, *The Closing of the American Mind*, New York: Simon and Schuster, 1987; Bellah et al., *The Habits of the Heart*, New York: Harper and Row, 1985). In my 1990 book, *Mosaic Madness: Pluralism Without a Cause*, I suggested that diversity becomes worth celebrating when we learn how to tap it for the collective good (Bibby, Toronto: Stoddart, 1990). It also can be argued that another reason we need to move beyond a pluralistic and relativistic view of the family is that such a posture has been resulting in our society tending to take a reactive rather than proactive approach to many family-related matters.

[42] The mutual respect that is required was expressed well recently by Suzanne Scorsone, the well-known Director of Communications for the Catholic Archdiocese of Toronto. Asked in an interview how Catholics can advocate the merits of heterosexual marriage, yet relate to homosexuals, her response was this: "When I hear people say we think marriage should be of a particular sort, that is one thing. When I hear other people say we want to fight gays as a group of people you don't do that. You don't denigrate human beings" (cited in an interview with Don Posterski, *Envision*, Summer 2002:9). I have no doubt that her hope would be that the feelings of the gay community are reciprocal.

[43] See, for example, Roderic Beaujot et al., *Family Over the Life Course*, Ottawa: Minister of Industry, 1995 and Zheng Wu, "Premarital Cohabitation and the Timing of First Marriage," *Canadian Review of Sociology and Anthropology*, 1990, 36:109-127.

[44] Roderic Beaujot, *Delayed Life Transitions: Trends and Implications*. Ottawa: Vanier Institute for the Family, 2004.

[45] See, for example, Statistics Canada, *The Daily*, March 17, 1998.

[46] Statistics Canada, 2001 Census, Catalogue nos. 95F0377XCB01003 and 95F0378XCB01004.

[47] Ms. Mesley is quoted by writer Sue Ferguson in a short insert of an insightful article by Katherine Macklem entitled, "Kids vs. Career," that appeared in *Maclean's*, March 15, 2004, pp. 24-29.

[48] Jane Jenson, "Against the Current: Child Care and Family Policy in Quebec." In Sonya Michel and Rianne Mahon (eds.). *Child Care Policy at the Crossroads: Gender and Welfare State Restructuring*. New York: Routledge, 2002.

Conclusion

[49] Tom Arnold, "Two-parent households are waning." *National Post*, October 23, 2002:A1

[50] This story was widely circulated by CP October 22, 2002. It appeared, for example, in *The Lethbridge Herald* on October 23rd, carrying the headline, "Canadian families growing less traditional."

[51] Erin Anderssen, "Junior's at home and grandma's alone." *Globe and Mail*, October 23, 2002:A1.

[52] Amy Cameron, "Ladies Not Waiting," *Maclean's*, December 23, 2002:42-43, and "Kindred Spirits Instead of Kin," *Maclean's*, January 13, 2003:44-45.

[53] Mary Nemeth, *Maclean's*, The Family, June 20, 1994. pp. 30-32.

[54] Robert J. Brym (ed). *Society in Question: Sociological Readers for the 21st Century*. Fourth edition. Toronto: Thomas Nelson, 2004:178.